Quick and Easy Crafts

Glass Painting

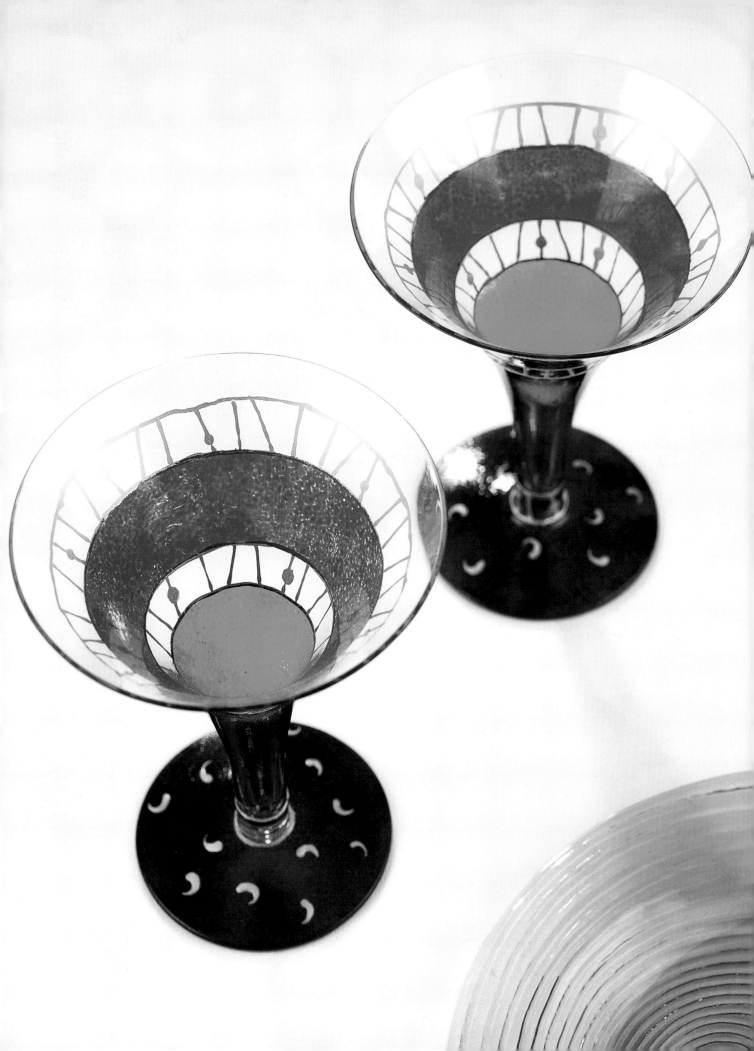

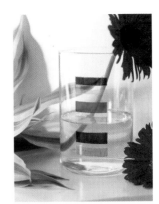

Quick and Easy Crafts

Glass Painting

15 step-by-step projects – simple to make, stunning results

CHERYL OWEN

NEW HOLLAND

This edition published in 2008 by
New Holland Publishers (UK) Ltd
London • Cape Town • Sydney • Auckland
www.newhollandpublishers.com

Garfield House, 86-88 Edgware Road, London W2 2EA, United Kingdom

80 McKenzie Street, Cape Town 8001, South Africa

Unit 1, 66 Gibbes Street, Chatswood, NSW 2067, Australia

218 Lake Road, Northcote, Auckland, New Zealand

ISBN 978 184773 462 4

Senior Editor: Clare Hubbard
Production: Hazel Kirkman
Design: AG&G Books, Glyn Bridgewater
Photographer: Shona Wood
Templates: Steve Dew
Editorial Direction: Rosemary Wilkinson

10 9 8 7 6 5 4 3 2 1

Reproduction by Pica Digital Ltd, Singapore
Printed and bound by Times Offset, Malaysia

Acknowledgements
The author and publishers would like to thank Pebeo (www.pebeo.com)
for supplying paint and outliner for use in the book.

Note
If you intend to eat off or drink out of a painted glass item, you should
check with the paint manufacturer that their product is suitable to be used
on such items.

Disclaimer
The author and publishers have made every effort to ensure that all
instructions given in this book are safe and accurate, but they cannot accept
liability for any resulting injuries or loss or damage to either property or
person, whether direct or consequential and howsoever arising.

Contents

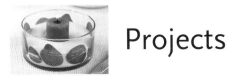 Projects

Introduction

The beautiful, translucent qualities of glass hold a fascination for many people and nowadays there is a superb choice of glass paints available to enhance that sparkle and gleam. Painted designs can be totally contemporary or imitate traditional stained glass styles.

If you are new to glass painting but have other craft hobbies, you will find that some of the techniques are similar to those of other popular crafts such as silk painting, stencilling and cake decorating.

This book has glass projects for the beginner and the experienced crafter. Lots of innovative techniques are explored and modern glass painting materials demonstrated. There are easy-to-use templates to help you get professional results. Once you have mastered using glass painting tools and materials that are new to you, enjoy experimenting and creating your own lovely designs.

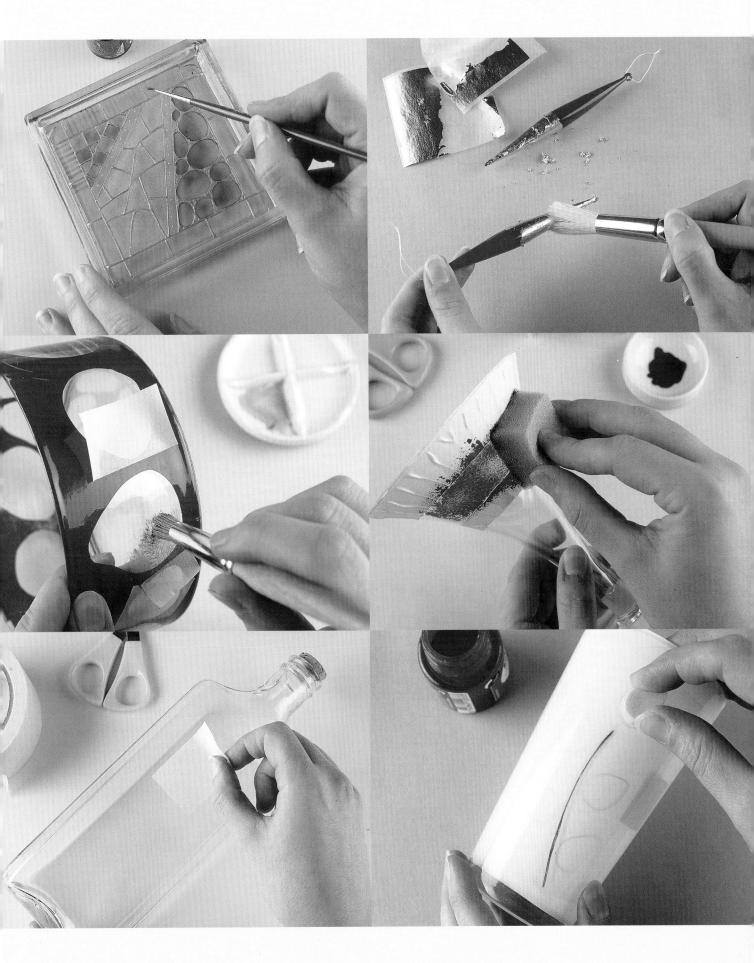

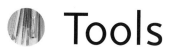 Tools

Specialist tools are not necessary for glass painting and you probably have much of the equipment needed already. Work on a well-lit, clean, flat surface and take care to keep sharp implements beyond the reach of children and pets.

Drawing

An HB pencil is the most versatile for drawing templates. A 2B pencil is good for transferring images. For accuracy, keep pencils sharpened to a point or use a propelling pencil. Use a ruler to draw straight lines. Draw templates that will be traced through glass with a black pen. Use a Chinagraph pencil to draw straight onto the glass. It gives a waxy line that adheres to the glass and can be wiped away easily with a piece of kitchen towel.

Cutting

Cut paper, masking tape and sticky-backed plastic with a craft knife or a pair of scissors. Rest on a self-healing cutting mat when using a craft knife and cut straight edges against a metal ruler. Change the blades often as a blunt blade may tear the paper surface. Store and handle knife blades carefully, they are very sharp.

Painting

A few good quality artist's paintbrushes such as a medium round brush, a fine brush, a flat brush and a stencil brush are the most versatile for glass painting and are used for all the projects in this book. Always clean brushes immediately after use. Wash off water-based paints in water and clean off oil-based paints with white spirit or a thinner recommended by the paint manufacturer.

Glass paints can be used straight from the container. Mix colours on a palette, an old ceramic plate or tile is ideal. Interesting effects are achieved by applying paint with natural and synthetic sponges. Moisten a natural sponge before use, use white spirit if using oil-based paints or water if using water-based paints.

Support curved glassware whilst you paint. Resting the glass on a few kitchen towels is often enough to stop a rounded item rolling around. A reel of tape is useful for sitting a curved piece on.

Many transparent glass paints are very runny. To stop paint running, support the painted area to keep it as level as possible whilst the paint dries. Resting the rim of a glass on an eraser is a useful tip as the eraser is a non-slip surface. Allow the paint to partly dry then turn the glass to continue painting. A hairdryer on a low heat setting held about 15 cm (6 in) from the work will speed the drying process.

Fine foam such as Neoprene is great for making stamps. Glue four layers of foam together and cut out the shape with a craft knife held upright, resting on a cutting mat.

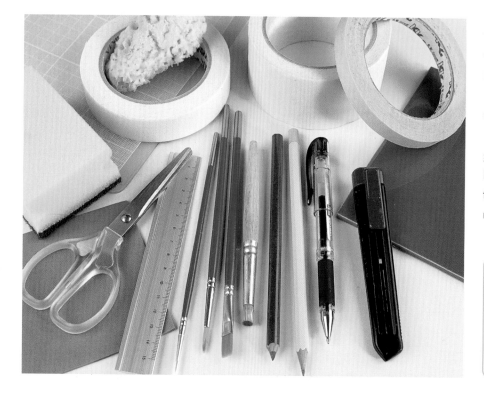

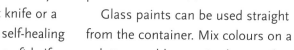

> ### Safety
>
> *When using any tools or materials always follow the manufacturer's instructions carefully.*

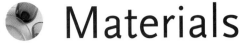 # Materials

Glassware

Practise painting on spare glassware such as old jam jars. Clear plastic packaging such as acetate is a good substitute when experimenting, but test an area first as the paint and plastic may not be compatible. Clear glass is suitable for all the techniques featured in this book. Coloured and frosted glassware are great to work on too. Faceted glass is fun to decorate as the angles can be outlined and sections painted. Recycling glass will also give an item a new lease of life, for example a slender bottle can become an elegant bud vase.

Clean glass well before painting. Wipe inside and out with methylated spirit using a soft, clean cloth. Stained or discoloured glass can be vastly improved with some varied remedies. One technique is to fill a glass container with denture cleaner dissolved in hot water. Another is to fill a glass container with white vinegar and sand, leave the solution for a few days, swill and then rinse. Alternatively, swill a couple of slices of potato in a stained container to clean it. Once the painted item is thoroughly dry, gently wash it in warm, soapy water before use.

Glass outliner

To imitate the leading in stained glass, glass paint is flooded within a raised outline drawn with glass outliner. The outliner is an acrylic paste that is piped from a tube. Outliner is available in gold, silver, copper, pewter, black and clear.

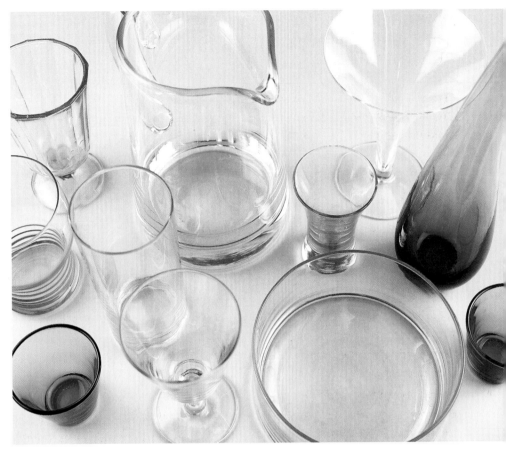

Masking tape

Templates can be stuck under glass with masking tape but it is most indispensable for masking off and protecting areas from paint. Masking tape is available in various widths. 2.5 cm (1 in) wide tape is the most versatile and 1 cm ($^1/_2$ in), 2 cm ($^3/_4$ in) and 5 cm (2 in) wide tape is also available. Tape can be cut in wavy lines or other shapes with a craft knife, either on a cutting mat and then applied to the glass or cut directly on the glass and the waste peeled away.

Sticky-backed plastic

Stencilling is a very popular pastime and can be worked successfully on glass using stencils cut from sticky-backed plastic. There is no seepage under the stencil because it is stuck securely. After stencilling, simply peel away the plastic to reveal the design.

Paints

Glass painting is an inexpensive craft. A little glass paint goes a long way and new shades can be created by blending colours. Remember not to mix water- and oil-based paints together. Most glass paints appear dark in their containers and painting swatches on acetate provides a quick source of reference to show how the paint will actually appear on the glass. Transparent and frosted glass paints are used for many of the projects in this book. Black and white glass paints are opaque and will make any transparent paint they are mixed with opaque too. To lighten a transparent colour, mix it with colourless transparent paint.

Ceramic paints are semi-transparent or opaque so they are distinct when applied to glass. Crackle-effect mediums give interesting effects. Experiment with other exciting mediums too, frosting medium will render transparent paints frosted and gloss medium will make paints extra glossy. An iridescent medium will create wonderful rainbow effects.

Glass painting pens are quick and fun to use and they come in a range of transparent and frosted colours. Shake the pens vigorously before use to make the colour flow to the felt-tip. Porcelain relief paint is piped from a tube and the colours are semi-transparent or opaque.

Many glass paints and pens can be baked to fix the paints. It is essential to use such paints if you intend to use the items to eat off or drink out of. Always follow the paint manufacturer's instructions and make sure the glass object that you are baking is oven-proof. The decorated glassware must be completely dry before baking, set it aside for at least 24 hours. Place the item in a cold oven then turn on the heat. This is usually 160°C (325°F) for 40 minutes. Turn off the heat and allow the glass to cool in the oven.

Glassware that has been baked is generally dishwasher-proof, but check with the manufacturer. Handwash decorated glassware that has not been baked in warm, soapy water.

The entire glass surface can be transformed with glass spray paints and frosted sprays. Use sprays in a well ventilated area and protect the surrounding area with plenty of sheets of newspaper or scrap paper. Designs can be masked off before spraying using masking tape or sticky-backed plastic.

Embellishments

Gilding is a fascinating craft and looks stunning on glass. Gold size is applied to the glass, allowed to become tacky then a fine layer of metal is applied to the size. Gilding is not suitable for use on functional items, it should only be used on decorative pieces.

For extra sparkle, stick cabochon jewellery stones to painted glassware using super glue. Use a gel super glue rather than liquid as it is easier to handle when just a small amount of glue is needed. It is best to use a pair of tweezers to stick small stones in position.

Safety

If you intend to eat off or drink out of a painted glass item, you should check with the paint manufacturer that their product is suitable to be used on such items.

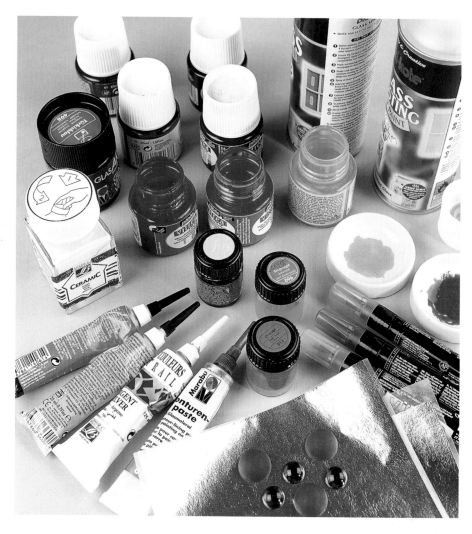

Techniques

The same basic techniques occur throughout the projects. Always read the instructions for a project before embarking upon it. Try out new techniques on spare pieces of glass. When referring to the instructions, use metric or imperial measurements but not a combination of both.

Using templates

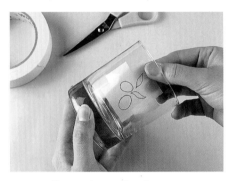

Trace-off templates for the projects are on pages 74–77. The templates for most projects can simply be traced onto tracing paper then taped to the inside of a clear glass item with masking tape and then worked on the right side. Trace onto tracing paper with a black pen rather than a pencil so the image is clear to see.

Transferring designs

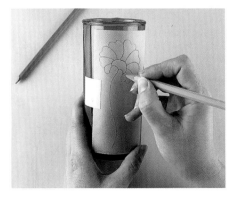

Opaque glass and narrow vessels cannot be traced through. Trace the template onto tracing paper then turn the tracing over and redraw it on the wrong side with a Chinagraph pencil. Chinagraph pencils are prone to blunt easily but it doesn't matter if the lines are thick.

Tape the tracing, Chinagraph pencil side down, on the glass. Draw over the lines with a sharp pencil to transfer the design to the glass. Any pencil lines that are visible when the glass is painted can be wiped away with a kitchen towel once the paint is dry.

To transfer a design onto the paper backing of sticky-backed plastic, trace the template onto tracing paper then turn the tracing over and redraw it on the wrong side with a soft pencil. Tape the tracing, right side up on the paper. Draw over the lines with a sharp pencil to transfer them.

Using a craft knife

Craft knives will give a neater cut than scissors. Cut on a cutting mat, cutting straight lines against a metal ruler and not towards your body. Masking tape and sticky-backed plastic are used to mask designs and fine foam is ideal for making stamps. They can all be cut with a craft knife.

Masking designs

Many designs are masked off with masking tape and sticky-backed plastic to create a smooth, even edge to your painting. Apply the tape to clean glass and press it down well so

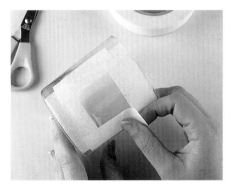

paint cannot seep underneath. Peel off the tape before the paint dries. This is not possible with all designs and dry paint may come away with the tape. If this starts to happen, press down the tape again and cut around the edges with a craft knife.

Applying glass outliner

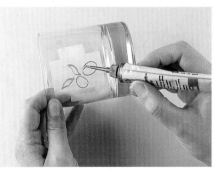

Squeeze the outliner tube gently as you draw it along the outline. Don't worry if the line starts with a blob, this usually happens! It can be neatened once dry, see page 13. When working on three-dimensional items, work on the uppermost area, allow to dry then turn the item to continue. Rest the glass on a few kitchen towels to stop it rolling around, or wedge rounded glass against another object to stop it rolling if necessary. Wipe the nozzle of the outliner tube on a kitchen towel when you have finished and replace the cap to prevent it drying out.

Tracing water level

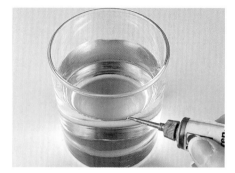

To apply level lines of outliner or paint to a vessel, stand it on a flat surface and pour water to the level required. Use the water level line as a guide to apply outliner or paint. Masking tape can also be positioned along the water level for masking designs.

Applying glass paint within outliner

Apply glass paint generously within an outlined shape (see photo below). A medium artist's paintbrush is the most versatile for painting. Use a fine

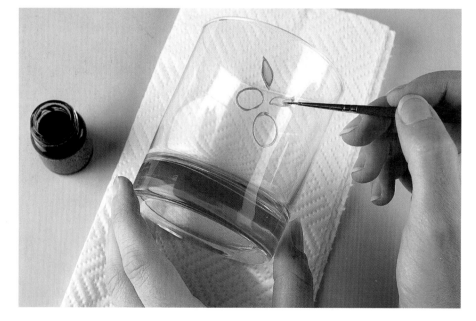

artist's paintbrush to push the paint into tight corners.

Shading with glass paints

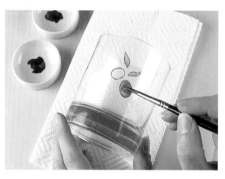

To shade colours on the glass, apply them separately then blend the colours together within the outliner.

Stencilling

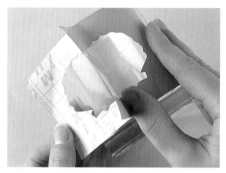

1 To make a stencil, transfer the design onto the paper backing side of sticky-backed plastic. Cut out the design with a craft knife, resting on a cutting mat. Place the stencil on the glass. Starting at one edge, gradually peel back the backing paper and stick the stencil smoothly onto the glass. Press it down well.

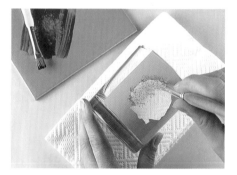

2 With a flat paintbrush, apply a thin film of glass or ceramic paint to an old plate or ceramic tile to use as a palette. Holding a stencil brush upright, dab at the paint to pick up a small amount then blot off any excess paint on a kitchen towel. Hold the brush upright to dab the paint through the cut-outs of the stencil, moving the brush in a circular motion. Peel off the stencil before the paint dries. A sponge can also be used for stencilling.

Sponging

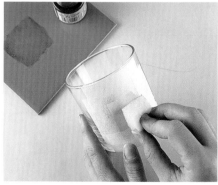

Depending upon the paint you are using, moisten a natural sponge with water or white spirit. Dab off the excess moisture on a kitchen towel. With a flat paintbrush, apply a thin film of glass or ceramic paint to an old plate or ceramic tile. Dab at the paint with a natural sponge for a random, mottled effect or a chunk cut from a synthetic sponge for an even coverage of paint. Alternatively, apply paint directly onto a synthetic sponge with a flat paintbrush. Press sponge onto glass to distribute paint.

Etching

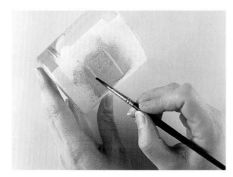

Etch simple designs in wet paint with a paintbrush or cotton bud. Wipe off the excess paint after each stroke.

Troubleshooting
Removing air bubbles and fluff

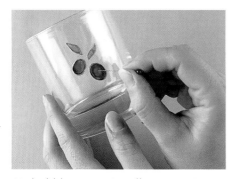

Air bubbles occasionally appear in paint. Wait a minute or two then pierce the bubbles with a pin to burst

them. Lift tiny pieces of fluff from wet paint with a pin.

Neatening outliner

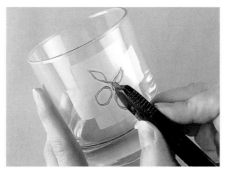

When the outliner has dried thoroughly, check to see if any areas can be improved. Although remember that once glass is painted, the eye will be drawn to the painted areas rather than the outline. Cut away the edges of any blobs with a craft knife. Do not neaten the line too much or it will lose character and appear to be applied by machine, just tidy up the more noticeable irregularities. Fill in any gaps in the outline with more outliner to prevent paint seeping through.

Paint not reaching outliner

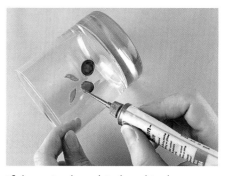

If the paint has dried and it does not reach the outliner in places, do not add more paint as it will give a noticeable ridge. Do not apply a second coat of paint as it will dissolve the first layer. Add a little more outliner to cover the area where paint is missing.

Removing paint
Dried outliner and paint can be scraped off with a craft knife before paint is fixed in the oven. Alternatively, clean it with a kitchen towel or cotton bud dipped in a suitable solvent for the type of paint you are using.

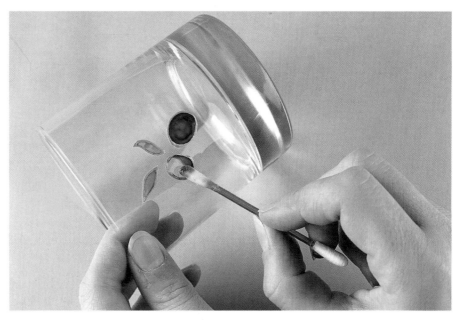

Striped vase

This vibrant vase with colourful stripes is a simple project for a beginner and is a good way of discovering how various transparent paints look when applied to glass. The neat edges are created by masking them off with masking tape.

Stripes work well in both traditional and contemporary room settings. Use colours to suit your home.

You will need

Materials

* Clear glass vase
* 2.5 cm (1 in) wide masking tape
* Pink, yellow, turquoise, light green, blue and orange transparent glass paints

Tools

* Scissors
* Cutting mat
* Craft knife
* Metal ruler
* 1 cm (3/8 in) wide flat paintbrush

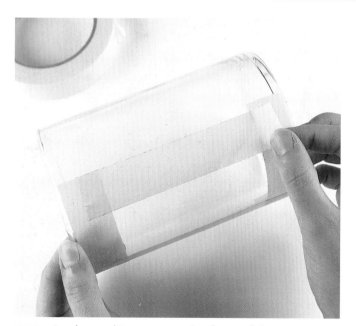

1 Apply masking tape to the front of the vase just below the rim and along the base. Apply vertical lengths of tape to the vase masking out a rectangle that is 4 cm (1½ in) wide.

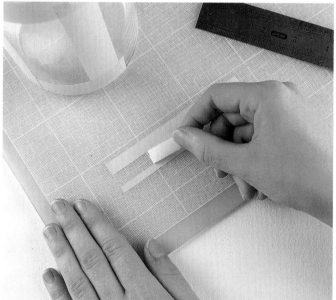

2 Stick a 12 cm (4¾ in) length of masking tape to a cutting mat. Using a craft knife against a metal ruler, cut the tape into two 5 mm (¼ in) and one 1 cm (3/8 in) wide strips. Cut the strips 6 cm (2⅜ in) long and peel them off the mat.

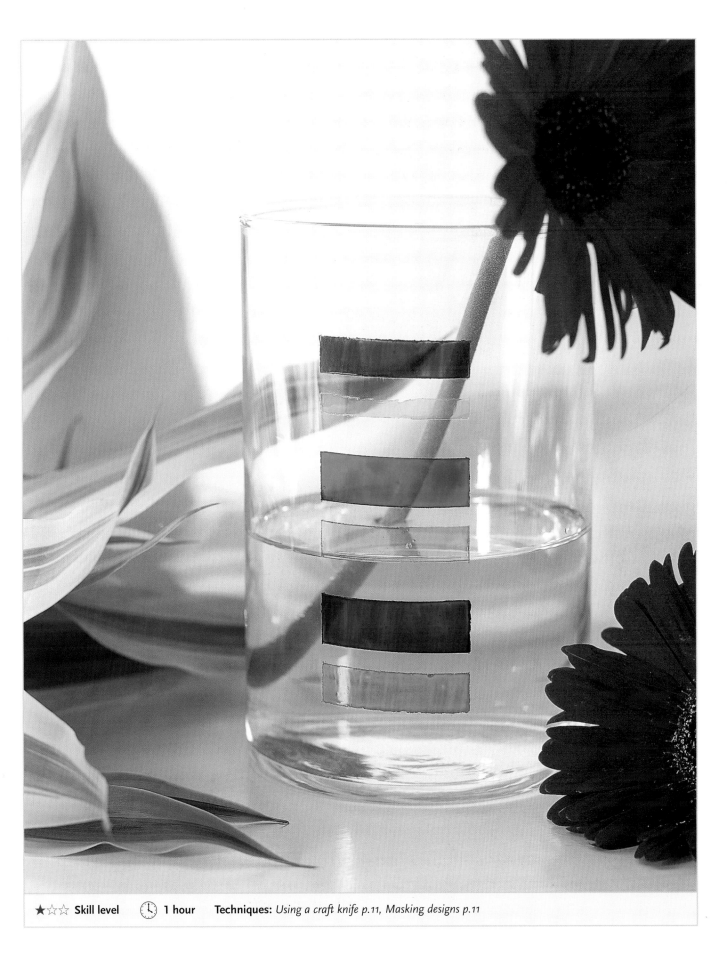

★☆☆ **Skill level**   🕐 **1 hour**   **Techniques:** *Using a craft knife p.11, Masking designs p.11*

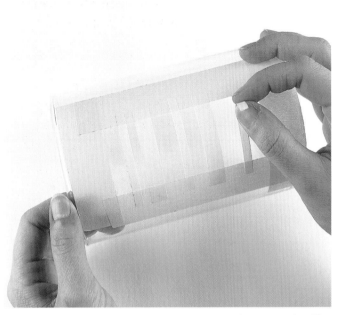

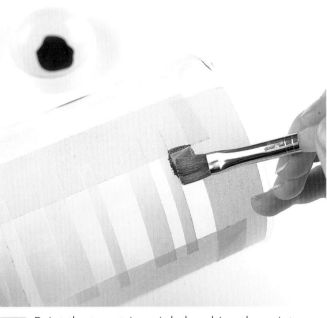

3 Stick the tapes across the rectangle to mask off six stripes of varying depths. Press the tapes down well.

4 Paint the top stripe pink, brushing the paint downwards.

5 Paint the other stripes with the other colours, brushing the paint towards the bottom of the vase each time.

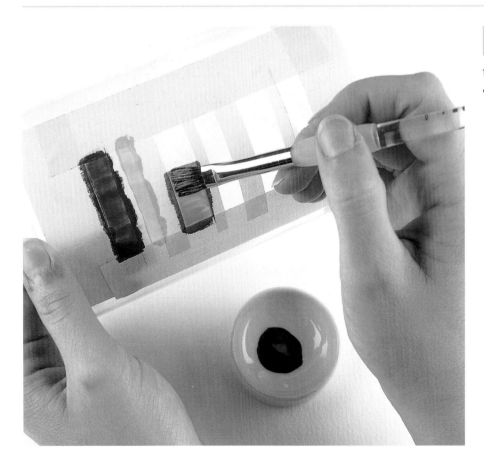

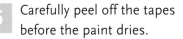

6 Carefully peel off the tapes before the paint dries.

Helpful hint
To avoid touching the wet paint when peeling off the tapes, lift the edges with the tip of a craft knife to start.

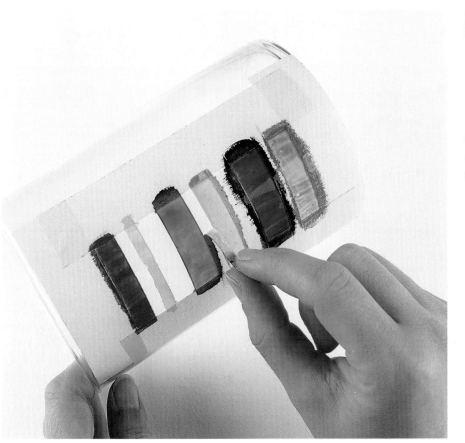

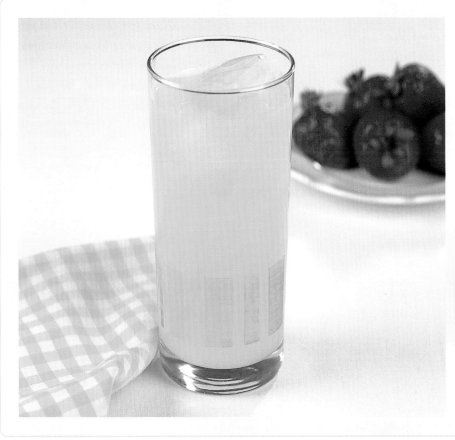

Variation

Frosted striped glass

Stripes also look good when worked all in the same colour. Apply stripes of frosted green glass paint around a hi-ball drinking glass.

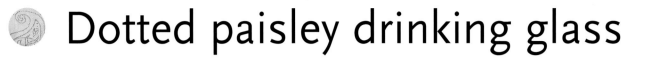

Dotted paisley drinking glass

This is a great project for a beginner. The pretty paisley motif is dotted with porcelain relief paint. The paint comes in a tube which is squeezed to apply it. Once the paint is dry, the vessel can be baked in the oven to fix the paint.

The paisley design is derived from Indian patterns. It gained popularity when finely woven shawls from Scotland featured the motif.

You will need

Materials
- Tracing paper
- Black pen
- Masking tape
- Oven-proof clear drinking glass
- Kitchen towels
- Orange porcelain relief paint
- Jug of water

Tools
- Scissors

1 Trace the paisley template on page 74 onto the tracing paper with a black pen. Stick the tracing inside the glass with masking tape. Rest the glass face up on a few kitchen towels to stop it rolling around. Dot along the outlines of the central design with orange porcelain relief paint.

Helpful hint
It is easier to apply dots than lines of relief paint. You may prefer to dot your own design freehand. If you are not happy with the result, just wipe it away and start again.

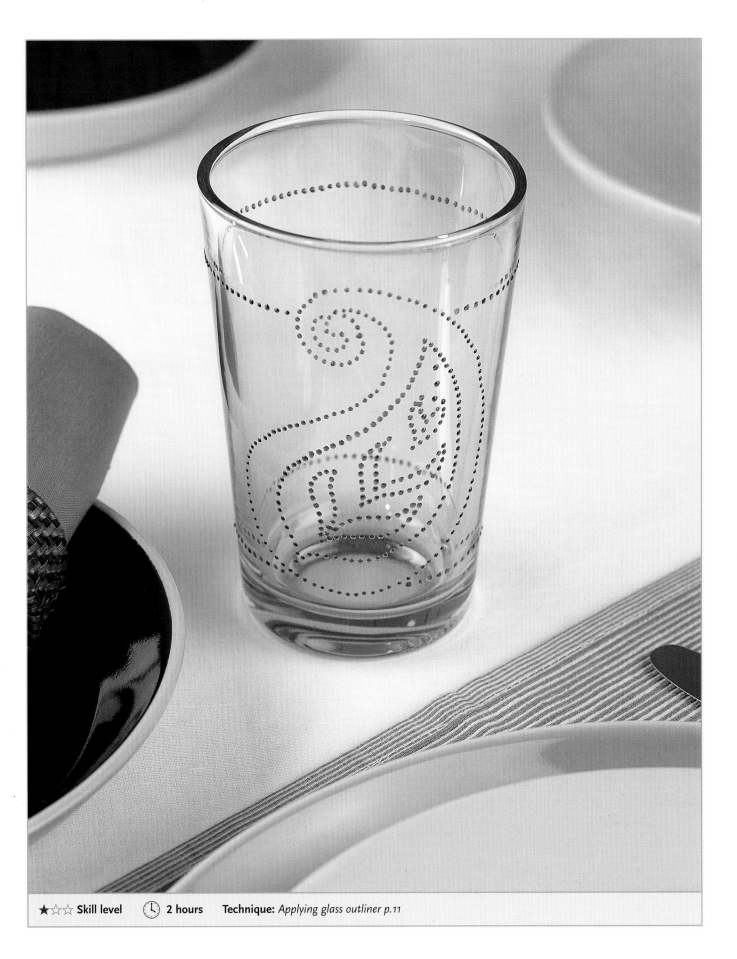

★☆☆ **Skill level**   🕐 **2 hours**   **Technique:** *Applying glass outliner p.11*

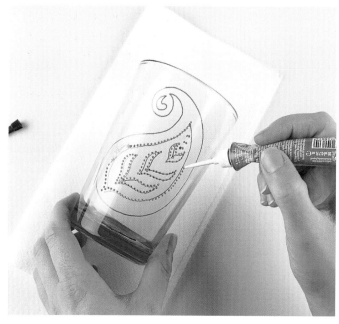

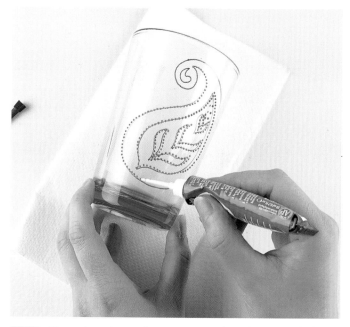

2 Working outwards from the centre so you are less likely to smudge the work, dot along the inner paisley shape.

3 Now dot along the outer paisley shape and the curlicue. Leave the paint to dry then stand the glass upright.

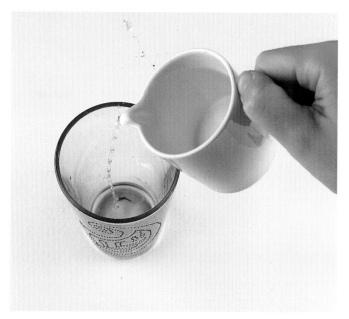

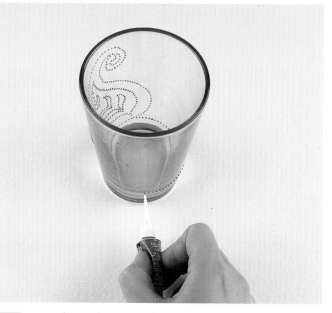

4 To mark a level line for the lower row of dots, pour water into the glass to a depth of 2 cm (³/₄ in).

5 Dot along the water line with the orange relief paint, breaking the line at the paisley motif.

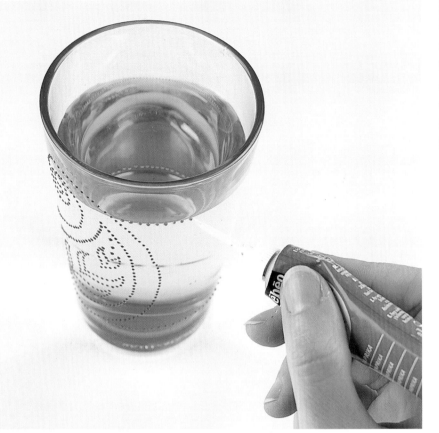

6 Top up the water to mark a line 2 cm (³/₄ in) below the rim for the upper row of dots. Dot the paint along the water line. Set aside for 24 hours then pour the water out and bake the glass following the paint manufacturer's instructions to fix the paint.

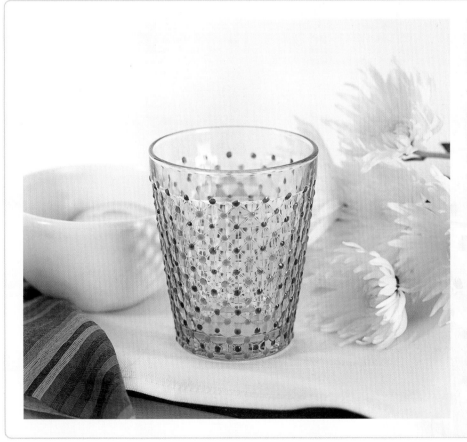

Variation

Dotted tumbler

This coloured tumbler is textured with a grid-like pattern which provides a useful basis for a regular pattern of spots of colours. Place a dot at each intersection of the grid, alternating yellow and orange porcelain relief paints.

Frosted shell jar

Etched glass is easy to imitate nowadays using glass frosting spray which is widely available at art and craft stores. A scallop shell provides the understated design on the front of this glass jar and a wavy border to the image suggests the ocean and continues the nautical theme.

This shell was created with a reverse stencilling technique where the surface surrounding the motif is worked on rather than the motif itself.

You will need

Materials

- 1 cm (½ in) wide masking tape
- Clear glass jar
- Tracing paper
- Sticky-backed plastic
- Scrap paper or newspaper
- Glass frosting spray

Tools

- Cutting mat
- Pen
- Craft knife
- Soft pencil

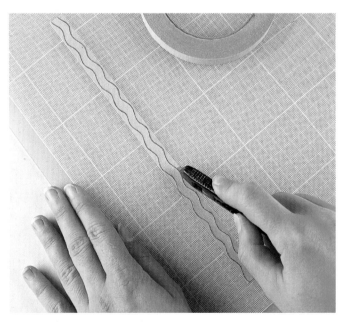

1 Stick a length of masking tape about 2 cm (³/₄ in) longer than the circumference of the jar to the cutting mat. With a pen, draw a wavy line just inside both long edges and cut out with a craft knife.

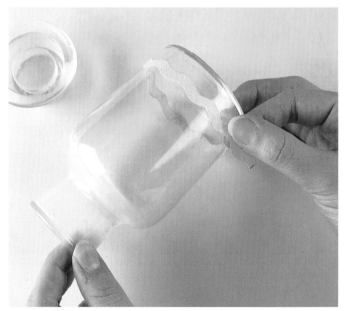

2 Stick the wavy strip around the jar 1.2 cm (½ in) above the base, overlap the ends of the tape at the back of the jar. Press the tape down well.

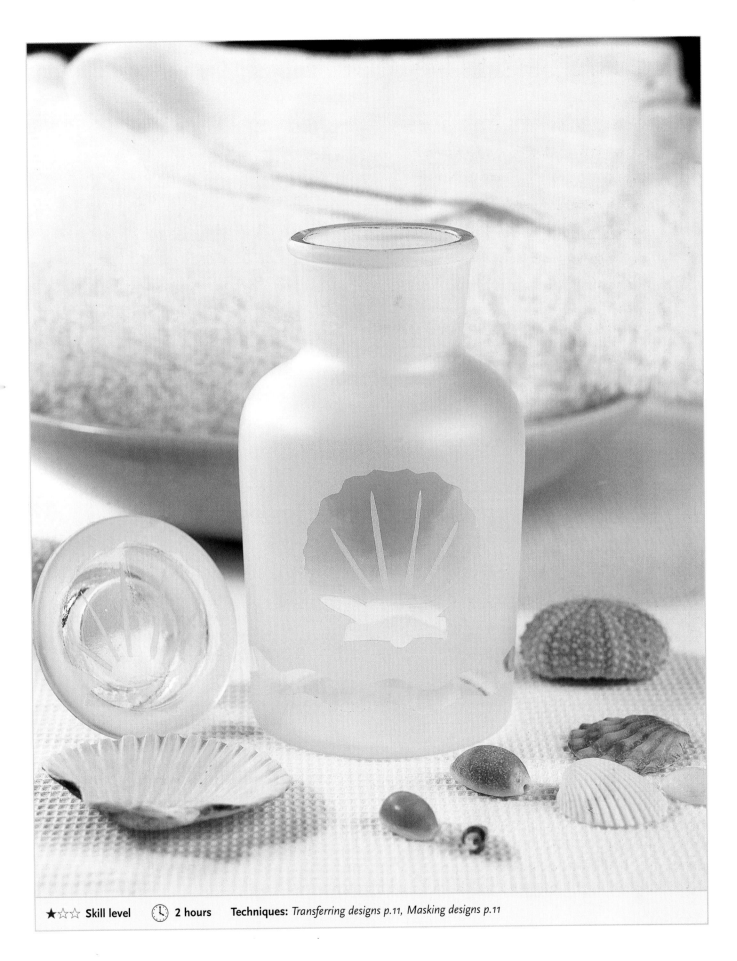

★☆☆ **Skill level**   🕐 **2 hours**   **Techniques:** *Transferring designs p.11, Masking designs p.11*

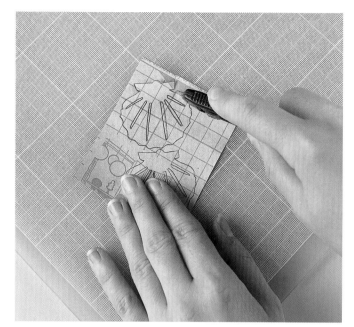

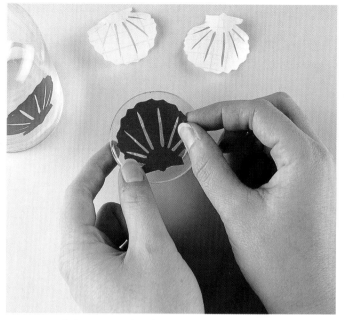

3 Trace the template on page 74 to transfer the shell onto the paper backing of a piece of sticky-backed plastic. Resting on a cutting mat, cut out the shell with a craft knife. If the jar has a chunky glass stopper, cut a shell for the stopper too. Cut out the ridge details on the shells.

4 Peel the paper backing off the shells and stick them to the front of the jar and centre of the stopper. Press the image down well so frosting spray cannot seep under the edges.

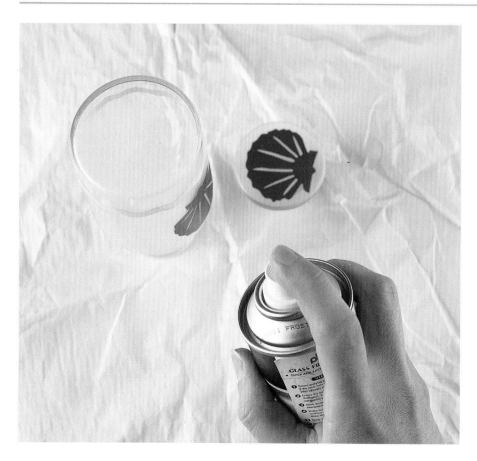

5 Cover the work surface with lots of scrap paper or newspaper. Turn the jar upside down and stand the jar and the stopper on the paper. Spray the jar and stopper with glass frosting spray following the manufacturer's instructions. The frosting will intensify as it dries.

Helpful hint
Build up the frosting on the glass in layers rather than in one go which may cause the spray to drip down the glass.

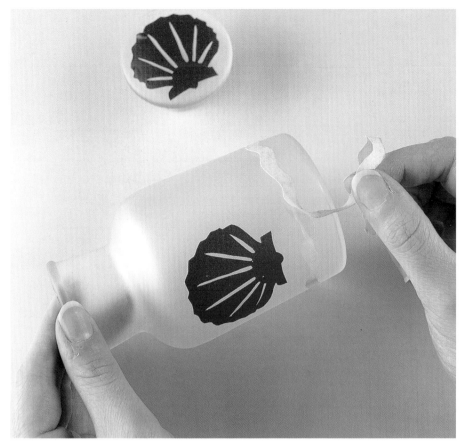

6 Leave the frosting spray to dry. Carefully peel off the plastic shells and tape.

Variation

Spotty vase

Apply round paper stickers at random to a shapely, clear glass vase. Spray with glass frosting spray and carefully peel off the circles.

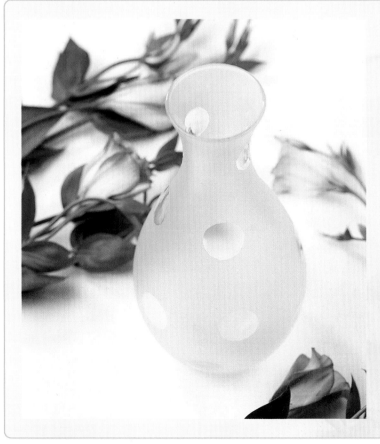

Floral bud vase

This delicate design of long stemmed flowers is worked with a fine paintbrush on a coloured glass bud vase. Bud vases are very narrow so a drawing cannot be stuck inside as a guide. However, you can transfer the design using a Chinagraph pencil (see page 74 for template). Alternatively, paint the simple design freehand.

The stems are worked in broken lines. This is easier to paint than single long, slender lines.

You will need

Materials
- Blue glass bud vase
- Kitchen towels
- Purple, white and blue ceramic paints

Tools
- Chinagraph pencil
- Fine artist's paintbrush
- Palettes

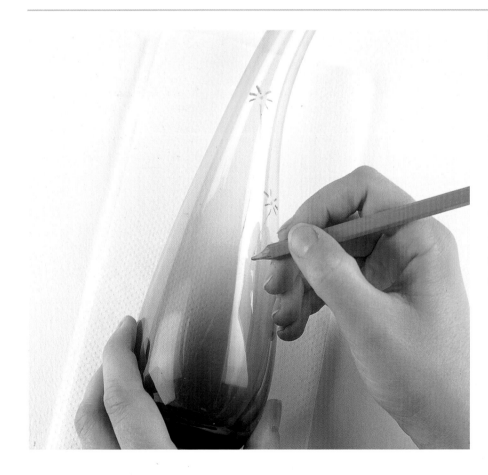

1 Rest the vase face up on a few kitchen towels to stop it rolling around. Use a sharpened Chinagraph pencil to draw the design on the vase. Draw long, sweeping lines for the stems.

Helpful hint
If you are not happy with your Chinagraph pencil drawing, simply wipe it away with a kitchen towel and draw it again.

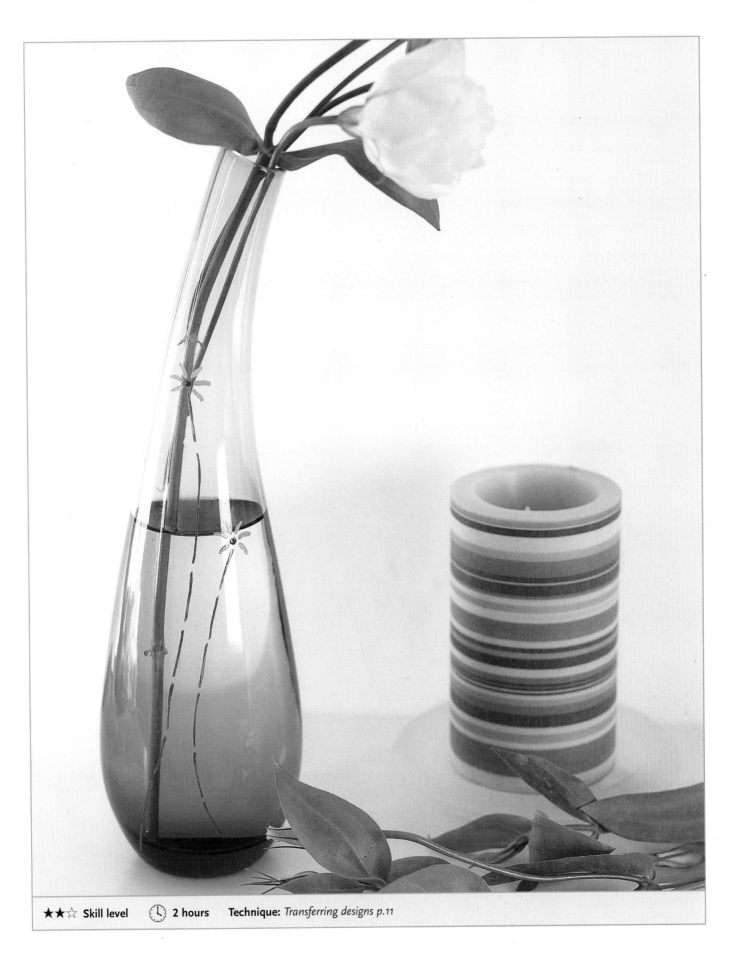

★★☆ **Skill level**   🕐 **2 hours**   **Technique:** *Transferring designs p.11*

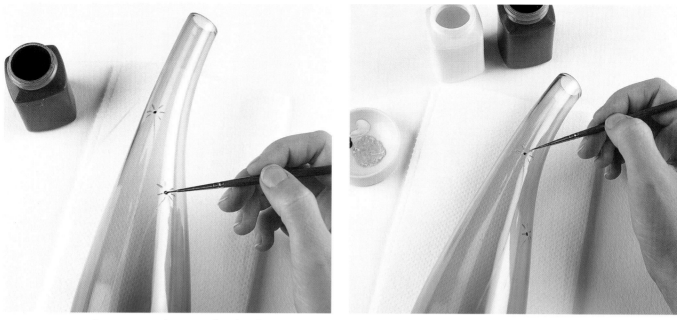

2 Dot purple paint on the vase for the flower centres.

3 On a palette, mix purple with a little white paint to make a lilac shade. With single brush strokes paint the petals of one flower outwards from the centre.

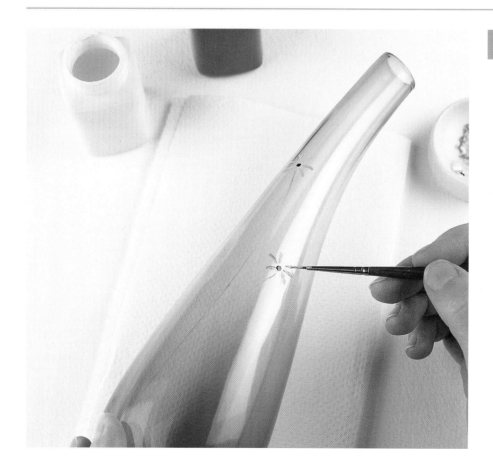

4 Paint the petals of the second flower in the same way.

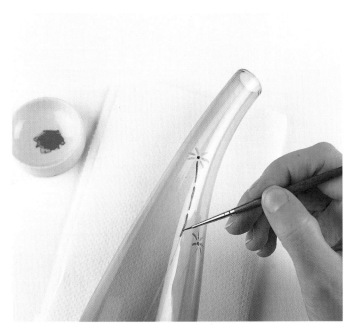

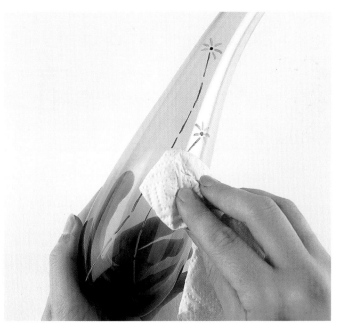

5 Mix purple, white and blue paint together. Paint the stem of one flower in broken lines about 2 cm (³/₄ in) long. Paint the stem of the second flower to match.

6 Leave the paint to dry overnight. Wipe away visible pencil lines with a kitchen towel. Bake the vase following the paint manufacturer's instructions to fix the paint if necessary.

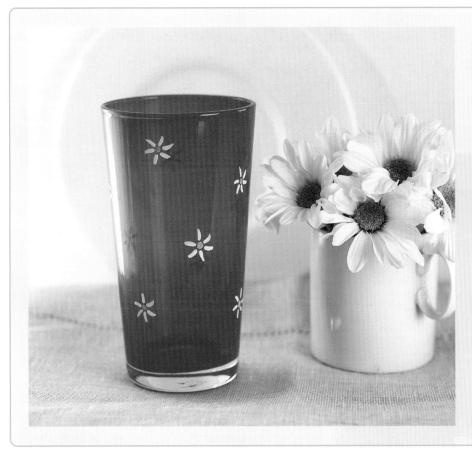

Variation

Daisy hi-ball glass

This charming daisy design is so simple that there is no need to draw it first. Dot yellow ceramic paint at random onto an orange drinking glass then paint white petals around each dot.

Seed-head plate

Inspired by nature, this fine seed-head is quick to work with a glass painting pen. The seeds are delicately dotted with frosted paints and a striped border encircles the image. The lively shades of light green and bright blue give a feeling of springtime, just change the colours to suggest other seasons, reds and oranges for autumn, for example.

For best results, paint the striped border with a flat paintbrush as it will give an even coverage and can be painted quickly.

You will need

Materials

- Tracing paper
- 1 cm (½ in) wide masking tape
- Oven-proof clear glass plate at least 23 cm (9 in) diameter
- Light green frosted glass painting pen
- Light green and bright blue frosted glass paints

Tools

- Black pen
- Palettes
- Fine artist's paintbrush
- Flat artist's paintbrush

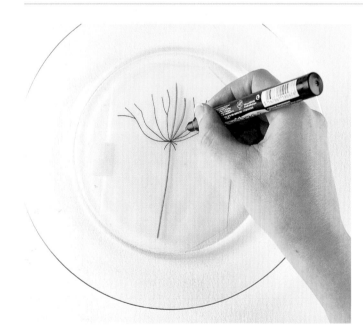

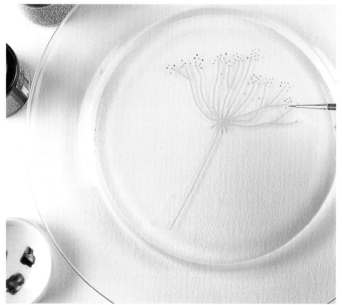

1 Refer to the template on page 74 to trace the seed-head onto tracing paper with a black pen. Tape the tracing under the centre of the glass plate with masking tape. Draw the stalks with a light green frosted glass painting pen.

2 Apply small amounts of light green and bright blue frosted glass paints to a palette. Mix a little of each colour together. Use a fine artist's paintbrush to dot the colours around the ends of the stalks to suggest seeds.

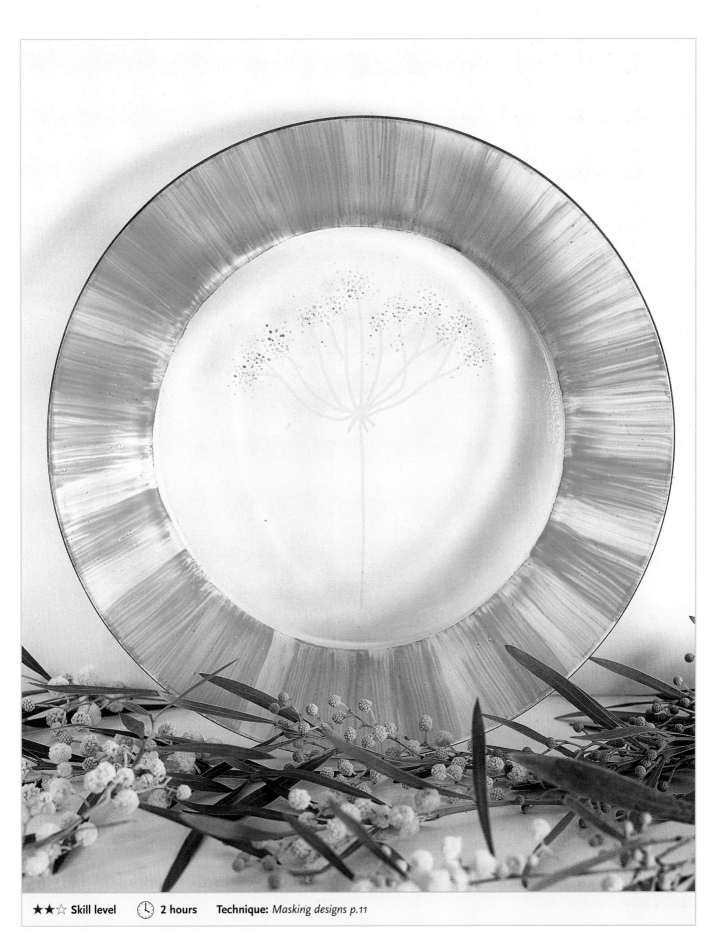

★★☆ **Skill level**   🕐 **2 hours**   **Technique:** *Masking designs p.11*

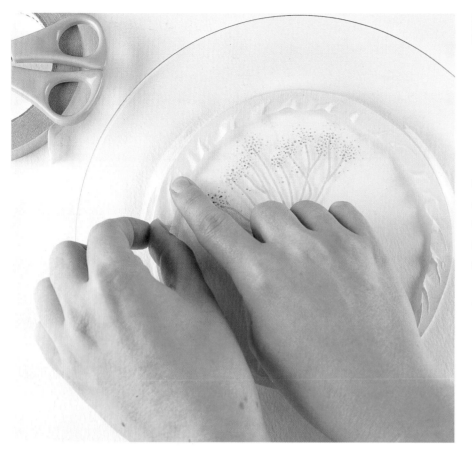

3 Stick a length of masking tape around the inner edge of the plate's rim. Press the tape down well.

Helpful hint
If the plate does not have a defined rim, measure in from the circumference of the plate the depth you require and mark it with a Chinagraph pencil. Join the marks to make a ring with the Chinagraph pencil. Apply masking tape along the drawn line.

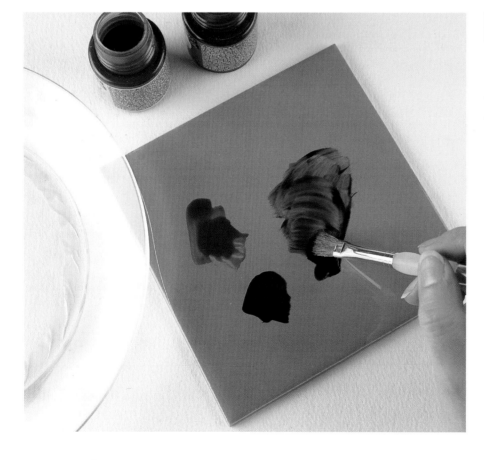

4 With a flat artist's paintbrush, apply more of the blue and green paints to the palette. Mix varying amounts of the two paints together to give you a few different tones to work with.

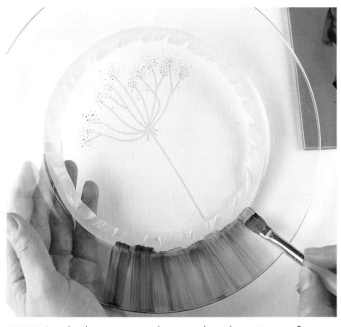

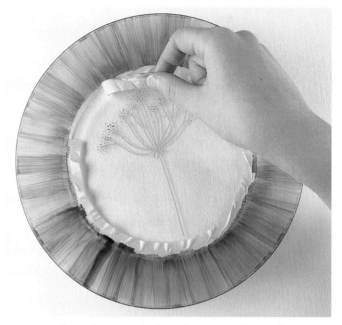

5 Apply the paint to the rim, brushing it out from the tape with a flat paintbrush. Brush one shade next to another to create subtly different stripes.

6 Peel off the tape before the paint dries. If necessary, bake the plate following the paint manufacturer's instructions to fix the paints.

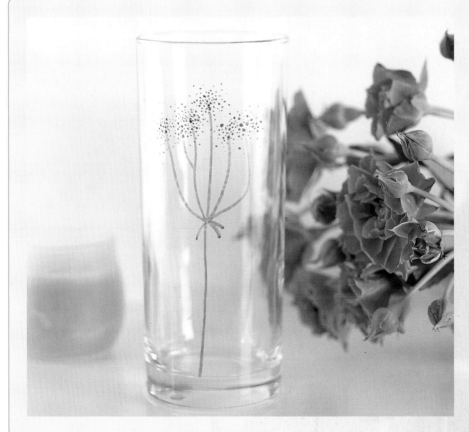

Variation

Seed-head glass

Draw the central area of the seed-head on a hi-ball glass with a turquoise frosted glass painting pen and dot the seeds with bright blue and pink paints.

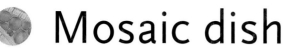

Mosaic dish

Mosaics are very popular and can be imitated by dividing the glass surface into squares or irregular shapes with glass outliner. Glass crackling medium was applied on some of these mosaics to give an aged, cracked effect. The crackling medium used here is applied in two parts then paint applied on top. Different manufacturers have different methods of application so read their instructions carefully.

This smart square dish is made of recycled glass and has a green hue which suggested the green and yellow colour scheme.

You will need

Materials

- Tracing paper
- Masking tape
- 11.5 cm (4½ in) oven-proof square clear glass dish
- Gold glass outliner
- Two-part glass crackling medium
- Light green frosted paint
- Yellow, deep green and light green transparent glass paints

Tools

- Black pen
- Medium artist's paintbrush
- Fine artist's paintbrush

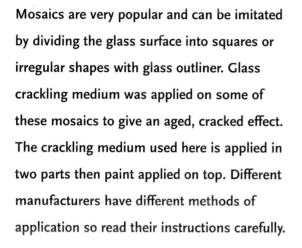

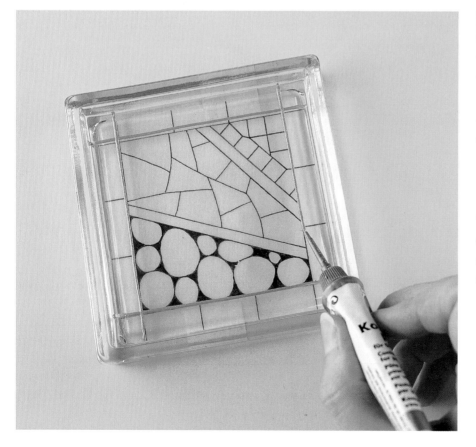

1 Refer to the template on page 75 to trace the mosaic onto tracing paper with a black pen. Tape the tracing under the dish with masking tape. Run gold outliner along the inner edges of the border of the design.

Helpful hint
Don't worry if you make mistakes with the outliner. They can be removed with a craft knife when the outliner is dry.

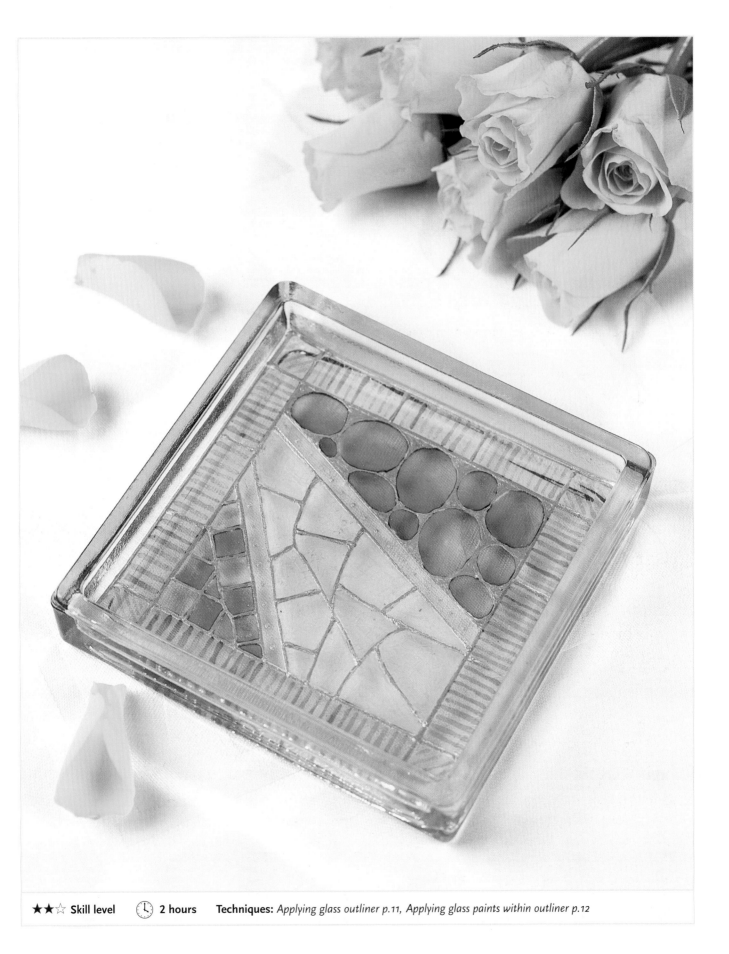

★★☆ **Skill level**   🕐 **2 hours**   **Techniques:** *Applying glass outliner p.11, Applying glass paints within outliner p.12*

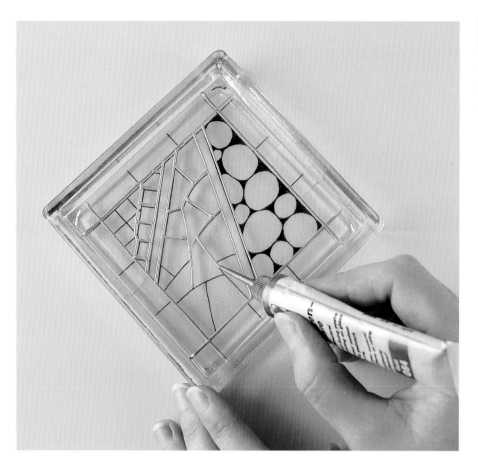

2 Apply the outliner to the design within the inner edges of the border and then to the outer edges of the border. Set aside to dry.

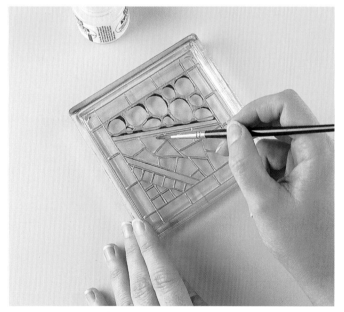

3 Apply the first phase of the crackling medium to the crazy paving mosaic with a medium artist's paintbrush. Set aside to dry, then apply the second phase on top. This will start to crackle as it dries.

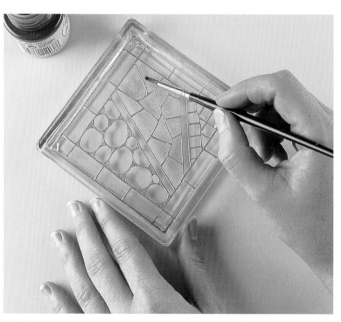

4 When the second phase is dry, paint the crazy paving with light green frosted glass paint. Apply the paint thinly to show the crackling effect.

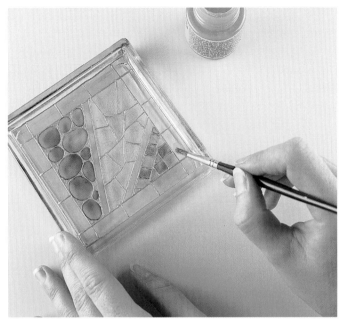

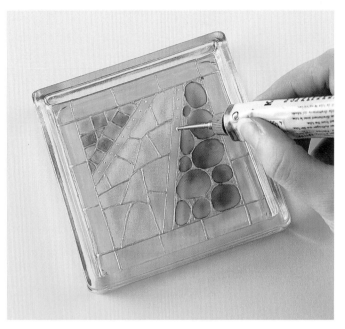

5 Paint the other areas with transparent glass paints; paint the border yellow, the pebbles deep green and squares a mixture of light and deep green. Leave the paints to dry.

6 Dot the outliner in a row along the inner rails.

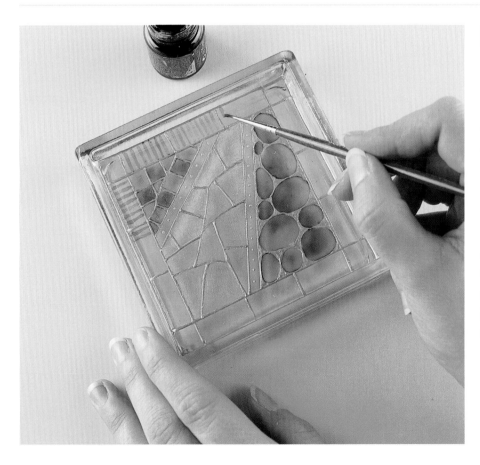

7 Use a fine artist's paintbrush to paint stripes across the border with light green transparent paint. Leave the dish to dry. If necessary, bake the dish following the manufacturer's instructions to fix the paints.

Helpful hint
The variety of small outlined shapes make this a great project to experiment with different effects such as embossing patterns in the paint or colouring mosaics with glass painting pens.

Gilded Christmas drops

Give some festive cheer to clear glass chandelier drops by colouring them with red glass spray paint and then adding a touch of opulence with gold leaf. Choose gold leaf with a paper backing, especially if you are new to gilding, as it makes the wafer thin metal easier to apply.

Gilded decorations are the ultimate embellishment for a special occasion.

You will need

Materials
- Thick sewing thread
- Selection of clear chandelier drops
- Scrap paper or newspaper
- Wooden or metal pole approximately 50 cm (20 in) long
- 2 old boxes or similar approximately 30 cm (12 in) high to support the pole
- Red glass spray paint
- Gold size

- Transfer gold leaf
- Gold thread

Tools
- Scissors
- Medium artist's paintbrush
- Soft brush

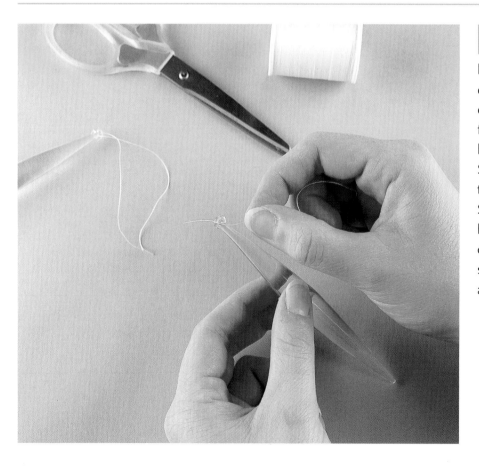

1 Insert a length of thick sewing thread through the hole at the top of each chandelier drop. Knot the ends together to create a loop to hang the drops from. Cover the work surface with lots of scrap paper or newspaper. Slip a wooden or metal pole through the loops of the threads. Support the ends of the pole on old boxes or something similar, placed on the scrap paper or newspaper, so that the drops are hanging just above the surface.

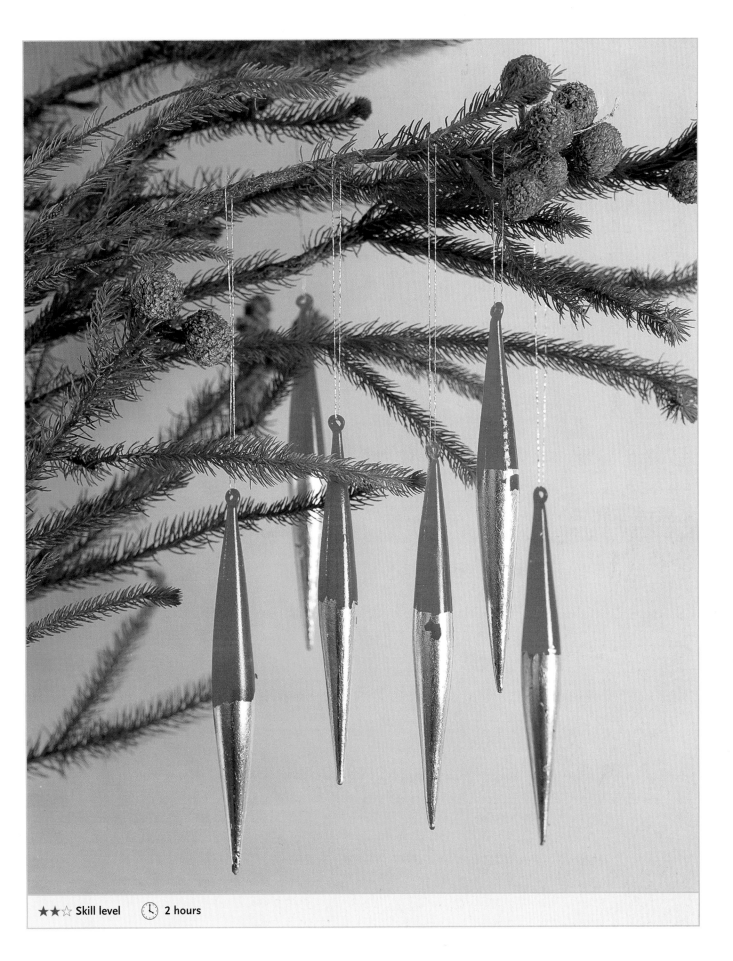

★★☆ Skill level   🕐 2 hours

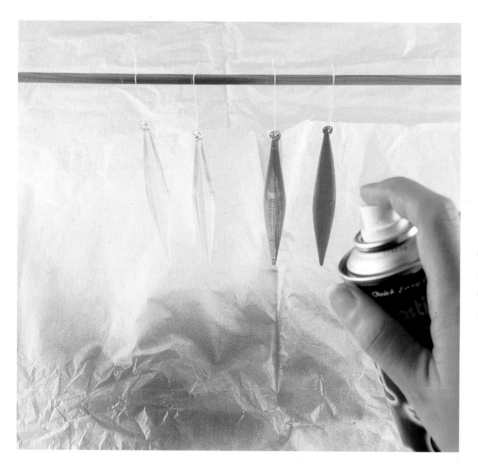

2 Spray the drops with red glass spray paint. Build up the colour gradually so the paint does not drip. Leave the paint to dry then turn the pole to spray the other side of the drops for an even coverage.

Helpful hint
The items used to support the pole when spray painting will be sprayed with paint too, so use old items or wrap them securely in plastic carrier bags for protection.

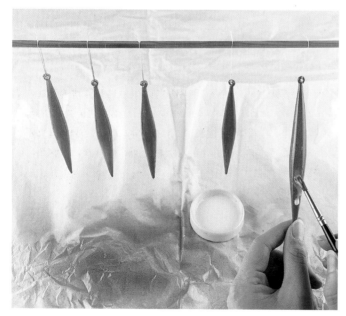

3 Leave the paint to dry, do not remove the drops from the pole. With a medium artist's paintbrush, apply gold size to the lower half of the drops. Leave for 15 minutes until the size feels tacky and has become colourless.

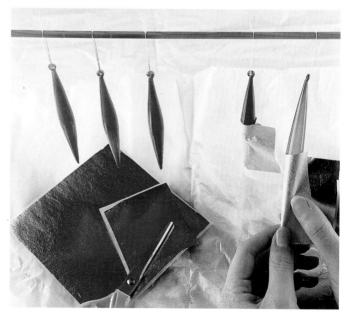

4 Cut a piece of gold leaf approximately 5 cm (2 in) square for each drop. Press the gold leaf around the lower half of one drop with the gold side against the size. Press the metal smoothly to the glass. Peel off the backing paper.

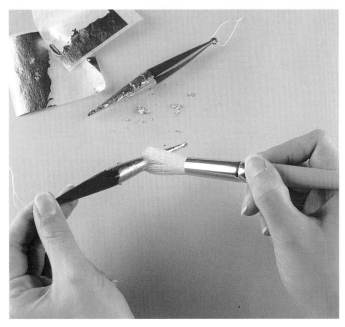

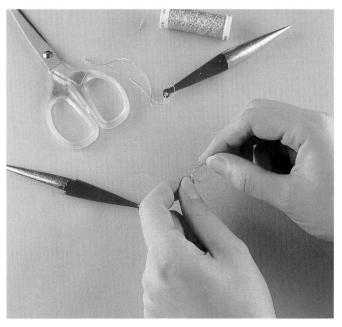

5 Use a soft brush to brush away loose pieces of gold leaf and to press the gold in place.

6 Slip the drops off the pole and cut off the sewing thread. Rethread the drops with gold thread.

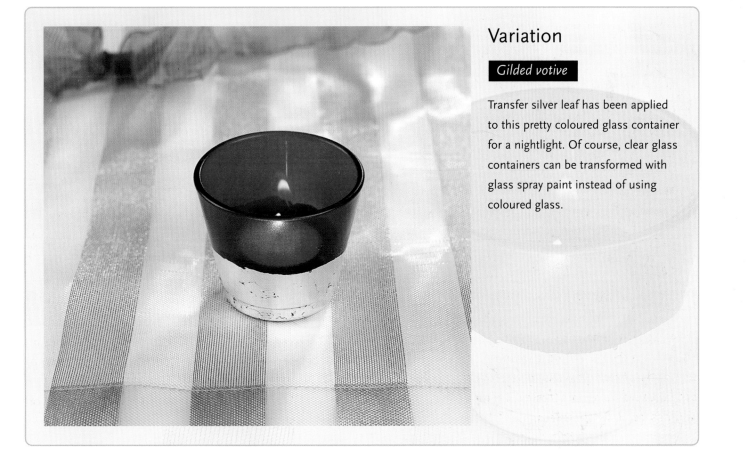

Variation

Gilded votive

Transfer silver leaf has been applied to this pretty coloured glass container for a nightlight. Of course, clear glass containers can be transformed with glass spray paint instead of using coloured glass.

Pebble bowl

The highly realistic pebbles encircling this glass bowl are very easy to create. The simple shapes are stencilled with ceramic paint and the shaded edges give a three-dimensional appearance. As a finishing touch, fine white fault lines, reminiscent of pebbles collected on beachcombing holidays, are painted across the pebbles.

Pebbles worked in a single colour look very effective when grouped together.

You will need

Materials

- Oven-proof clear glass straight-sided bowl at least 6 cm (2½ in) high
- Sticky-backed plastic
- Masking tape
- White, black, yellow ochre, green and pink ceramic paints
- Kitchen towel
- Cotton bud (optional)
- White spirit (optional)

Tools

- Tape measure
- Craft knife
- Cutting mat
- Metal ruler
- Pencil
- Medium artist's paintbrush
- Palette
- Stencil brush
- Fine artist's paintbrush

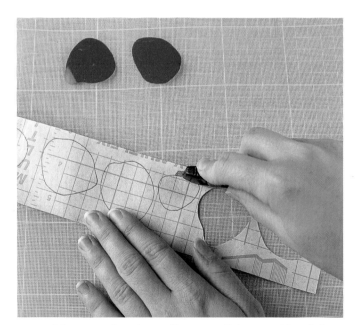

1 Measure the circumference of the outside of the bowl with a tape measure. Cut a 6 cm (2½ in) wide strip of sticky-backed plastic to fit around the outside of the bowl. Refer to the template on page 75 to draw a row of pebbles along the strip. Resting on a cutting mat, cut out the pebbles with a craft knife.

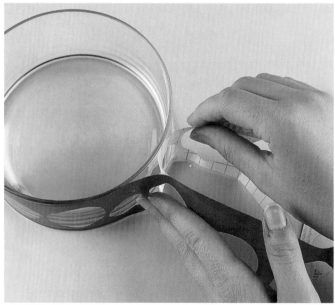

2 Make sure the bowl is clean then peel back one end of the paper backing of the strip. Stick the strip around the bowl, peeling off the backing paper as you go. Press the strip down well.

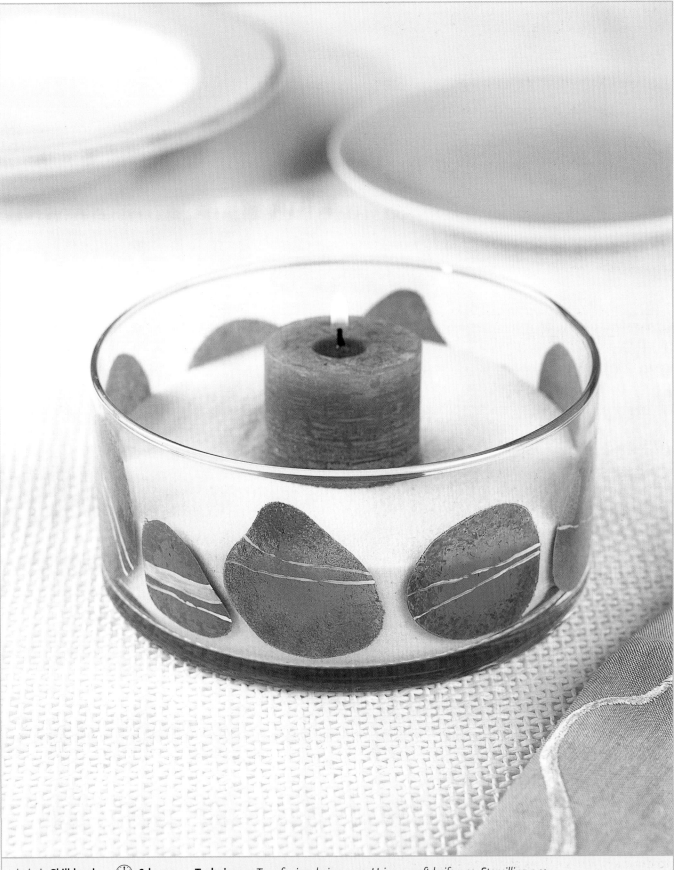

★★★ **Skill level**   🕐 **3 hours**   **Techniques:** *Transferring designs p.11, Using a craft knife p.11, Stencilling p.12*

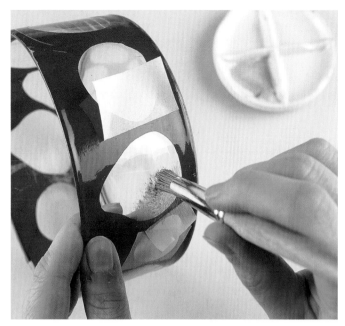

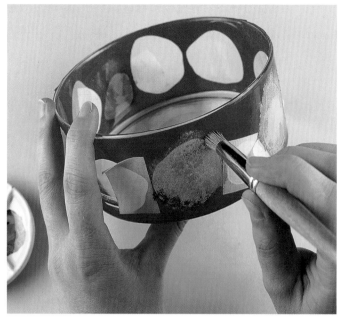

3 Mask off one pebble. With a medium artist's paintbrush, mix white with a little black ceramic paint to make grey. Pick up a little of the paint with a stencil brush. Dab off the excess on a kitchen towel. Dab the paint through the stencil, moving the brush in a circular motion. Stencil a few more pebbles grey.

4 Mix a little more black paint with the grey to darken it. Stencil the darker shade sparingly around the edges of the painted pebbles.

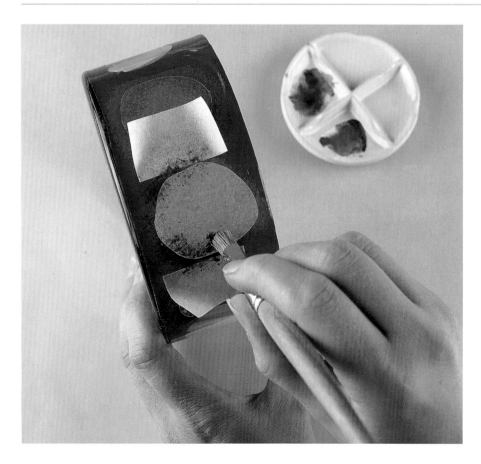

5 Now mix yellow ochre with white and a little black paint to make a dull yellow shade; then green paint with white and a little black. Stencil a few more pebbles, masking off the surrounding pebbles with masking tape as before. Do not stick the tape to the painted surface, just to the sticky-backed plastic. Mix in a little more black paint to darken the yellow and green shades. Stencil the darker shade sparingly around the edges of the pebbles.

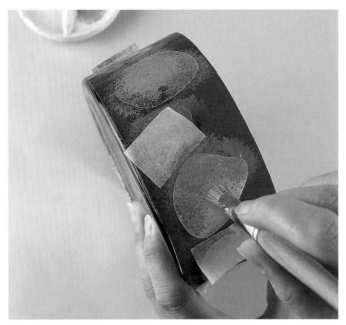

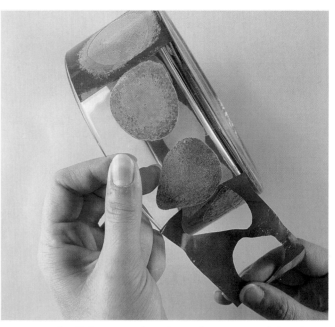

6 Mix pink with white and a little black paint. Stencil the remaining pebbles, masking off the surrounding ones. Mix in a little more black paint to darken the pink and shade the outer edges as before.

7 Peel off the stencil and masking tape whilst the paint is still wet. Leave the bowl to dry.

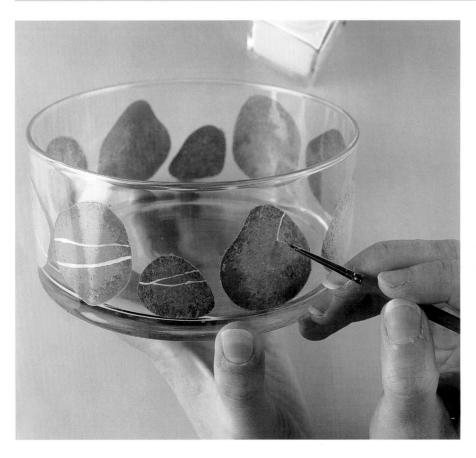

8 Paint lines freehand across the pebbles with white paint, using a fine artist's paintbrush. If necessary, set aside for 24 hours then bake the bowl following the paint manufacturer's instructions to fix the paints.

Helpful hint

Wipe away any adhesive left from the sticky-backed plastic with a cotton bud dipped in white spirit once the paints are dry.

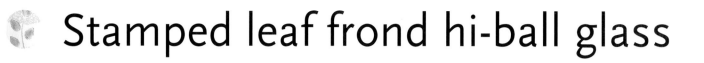

Stamped leaf frond hi-ball glass

A stamp cut from fine foam is used to stamp leaves with frosted glass paint on this charming drinking glass. The stamping technique gives a subtle texture which is very effective on the white glass. Decorative bands made using frosted glass painting pens encircle the glass.

This technique would also work on clear glass but avoid brightly coloured glass as the effect will not show up.

You will need

Materials
- Tracing paper
- 2.5 cm (1 in) wide masking tape
- Oven-proof white drinking glass
- Kitchen towels
- Pink frosted glass paint
- Fine foam
- All-purpose household glue
- Jug of water
- Light green and turquoise frosted glass painting pens

Tools
- Black pen
- Fine artist's paintbrush
- Cutting mat
- Craft knife
- Metal ruler
- Flat artist's paintbrush

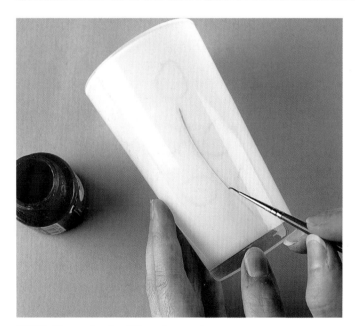

1 Trace the leaf frond template on page 75 onto tracing paper with a black pen, also trace a single leaf and set it aside. Tape the tracing inside the glass with masking tape. Rest the glass face up on a few kitchen towels. Using a fine artist's paintbrush, paint the stalk with pink frosted glass paint.

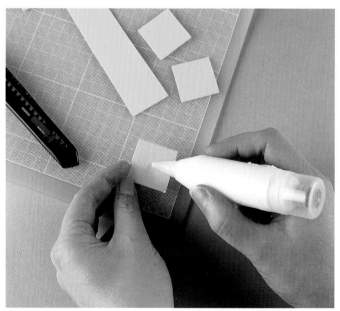

2 Resting on a cutting mat, cut four 3 cm (1¼ in) squares of foam with a craft knife against a metal ruler. Glue the squares one on top of the other to make a block. Set the block aside whilst the glue dries.

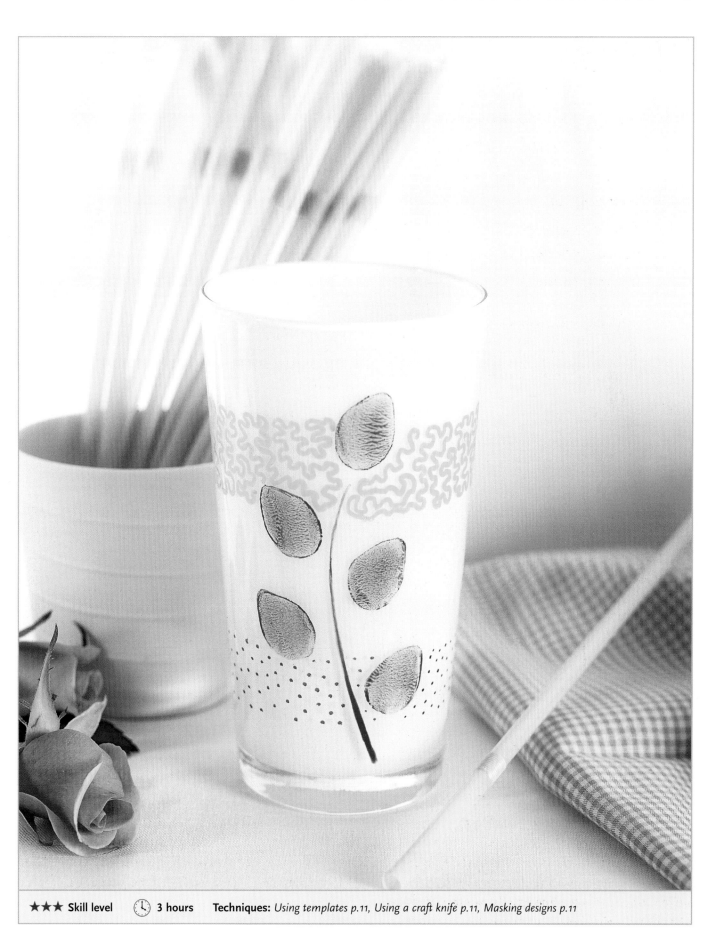

★★★ **Skill level**　🕐 **3 hours**　**Techniques:** *Using templates p.11, Using a craft knife p.11, Masking designs p.11*

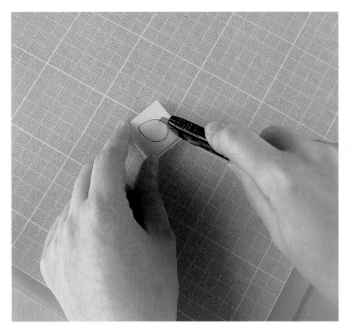

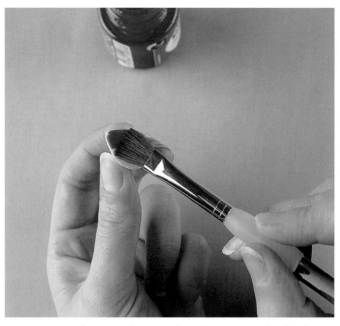

3 Cut out the single leaf template, place in the centre of the foam block and draw around it. Place the block on a cutting mat and, holding the knife vertically, cut the leaf shape out of the block to make a stamp.

4 Use a flat artist's paintbrush to paint the leaf stamp pink.

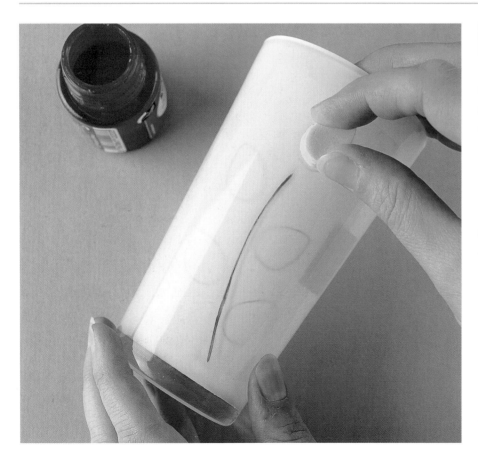

5 Press the leaf stamp firmly onto the glass at the top leaf position. Lift the stamp off smoothly then repaint it to stamp each remaining leaf in the same way. Leave the glass to dry.

Helpful hint
Immediately wipe away the edges of stamped leaves that have smudged with a moistened fine paintbrush.

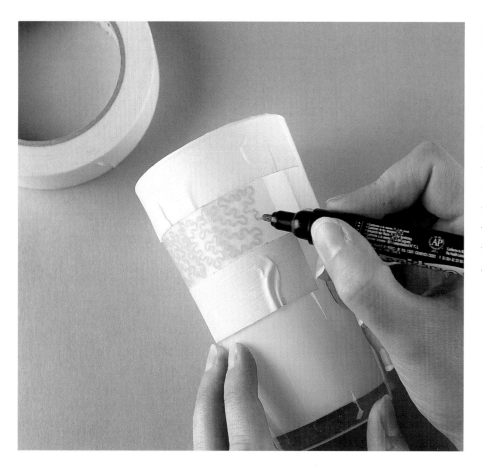

6 Apply a length of masking tape around the top of the glass, starting and stopping each side of the top leaf. Pour water into the glass to 2.5 cm (1 in) below the tape and use the water level as a guide to apply a second length of tape, avoiding the leaves as before. Pour out the water. Draw a freehand squiggle pattern within the masked edges with a light green frosted glass painting pen. Leave to dry then peel off the masking tape.

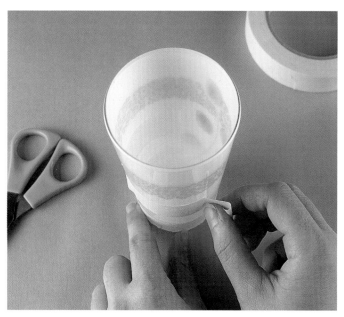

7 Apply a length of masking tape around the bottom of the glass, starting and stopping each side of the stem. Pour water into the glass to 2 cm (³/₄ in) above the tape and use the water level as a guide to apply a second length of tape, avoiding the leaves as before. Pour out the water.

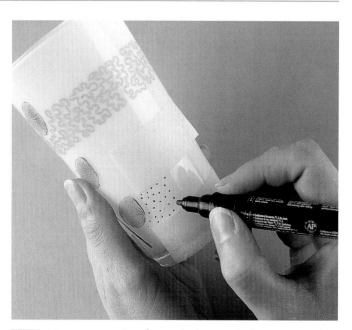

8 Use a turquoise frosted glass painting pen to dot the glass randomly within the masked edges. Peel off the masking tape. If necessary, bake the glass following the paint manufacturer's instructions to fix the paints.

Stamped and etched shot glasses

Bold circles in bright, cheery colours are stamped on this set of shot glasses with a synthetic sponge. Designs are etched in the paint with a paintbrush before the paint dries. You could use this method to decorate other sets of glasses, plates and dishes.

Experiment etching with other sizes of paintbrushes to create different widths of line.

You will need

Materials

* Waterproof pen
* Synthetic sponge
* Aquamarine, yellow, orange and pink ceramic paints
* Four oven-proof shot glasses

Tools

* Cutting mat
* Craft knife
* Flat artist's paintbrush
* Medium artist's paintbrush

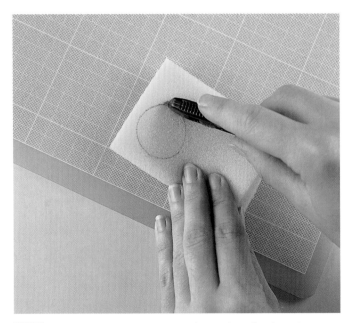

1 Draw a 3 cm (1¼ in) circle (either freehand or draw around a coin etc.) on a synthetic sponge with a waterproof pen. (If you are using a kitchen sponge backed with a scourer, draw the circle on the scourer.) Resting on a cutting mat, cut out the circle with a craft knife, holding the knife vertically.

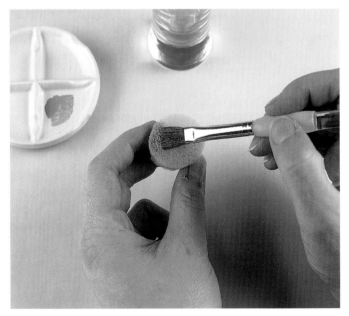

2 Paint the face of the sponge with aquamarine ceramic paint using a flat paintbrush.

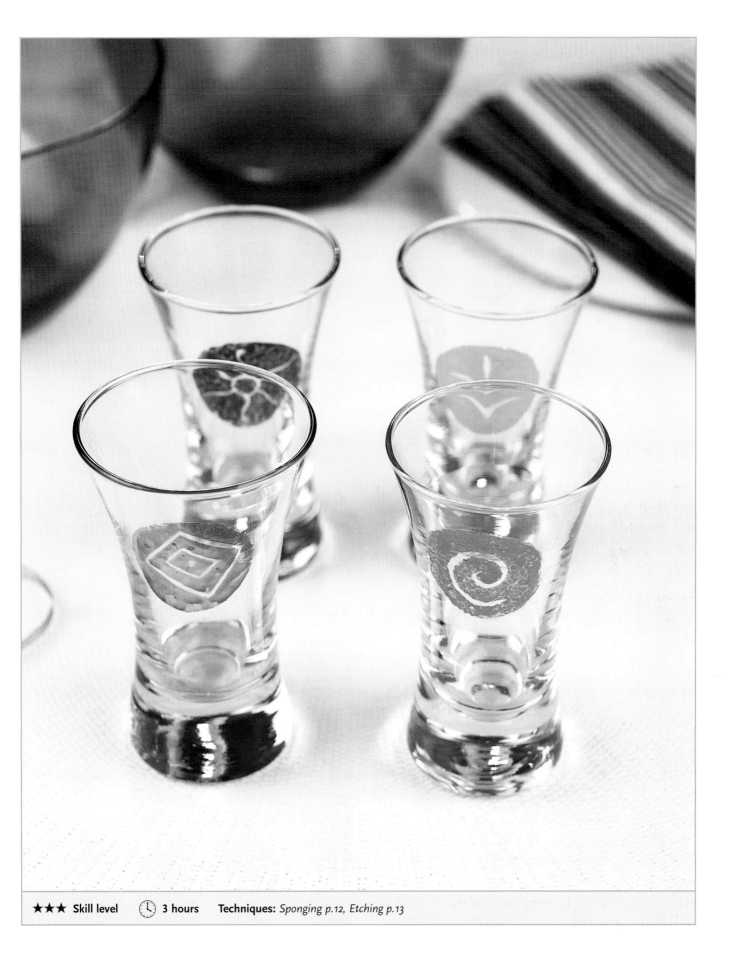

★★★ **Skill level**   🕐 **3 hours**   **Techniques:** *Sponging p.12, Etching p.13*

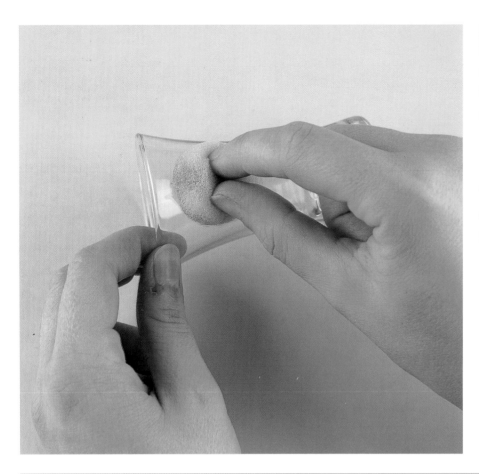

3 Press the sponge onto a shot glass 1 cm (³/8 in) below the rim applying firm pressure. Rock the sponge slightly to apply the paint over the curved surface.

Helpful hint
If the stamped circle is uneven, neaten the edges with a moistened paintbrush before the paint dries.

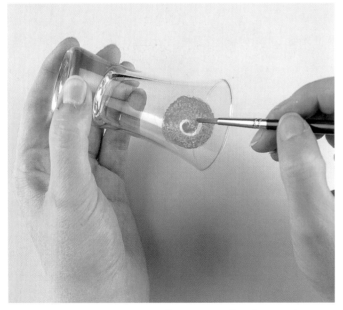

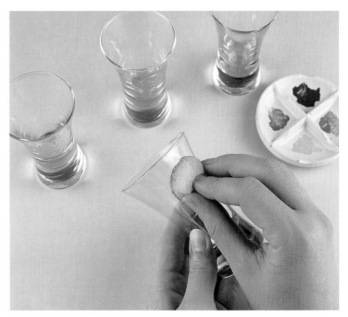

4 While the paint is still wet, use the dry medium paintbrush to draw a spiral within the circle. Wipe the excess paint off the brush. Clean and dry the sponge before continuing.

5 Stamp another shot glass in a different colour. Etch another design with the medium paintbrush.

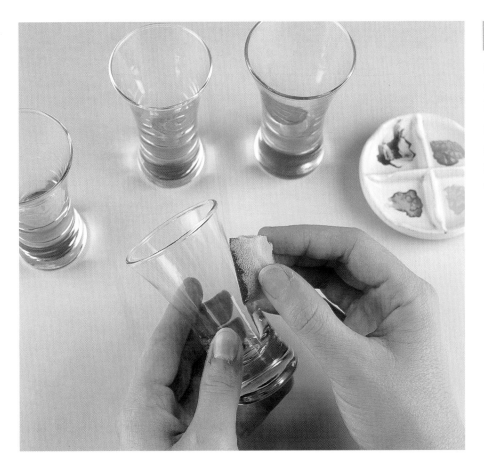

6 Continue stamping the glasses in contrasting colours and etching a different design in each. I've used diamonds, swirls, leaves and sun shapes. Leave the paint overnight then bake the glasses following the paint manufacturer's instructions to fix the paints.

Variation

Leaf wine glass

Cut a leaf shape from a sponge and stamp at random onto a wine glass with green ceramic paint. Etch veins in the wet paint with a medium paintbrush.

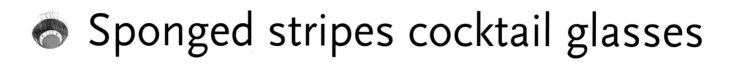

Sponged stripes cocktail glasses

Toast a special celebration with these vividly coloured cocktail glasses. The bands of colour are applied with a synthetic sponge and the details are added with gold glass outliner.

Add highlights to glassware by applying outliner on top of a painted surface.

You will need

Materials

- 2.5 cm (1 in) and 1 cm (½ in) wide masking tape
- Ovenproof clear glass cocktail glasses
- Jug of water
- Pink, turquoise and purple transparent glass paint
- Synthetic sponge
- Gold glass outliner

Tools

- Scissors
- Ruler
- Flat artist's paintbrush
- Fine artist's paintbrush

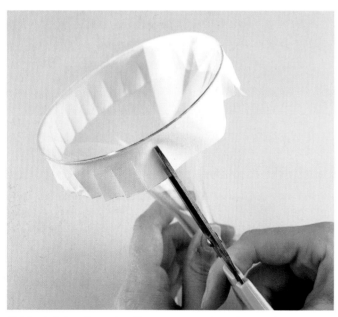

1 Stick a length of 2.5 cm (1 in) wide masking tape around the rim of the cocktail glass, pressing the tape to the rim only. Snip into the tape at approximately 1 cm (½ in) intervals to fit it to the sloping glass. Press the tape to the glass, smoothing it downwards from the rim.

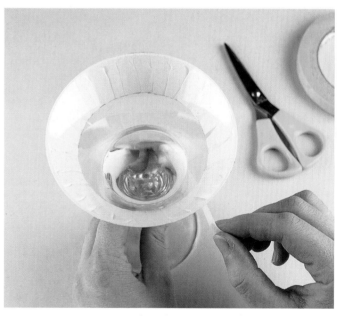

2 Pour water into the glass until it is 2.5 cm (1 in) below the tape. Use this as a guide to stick a length of narrow tape around the glass. Press the tape down in random pleats on the angled surface. Pour away the water.

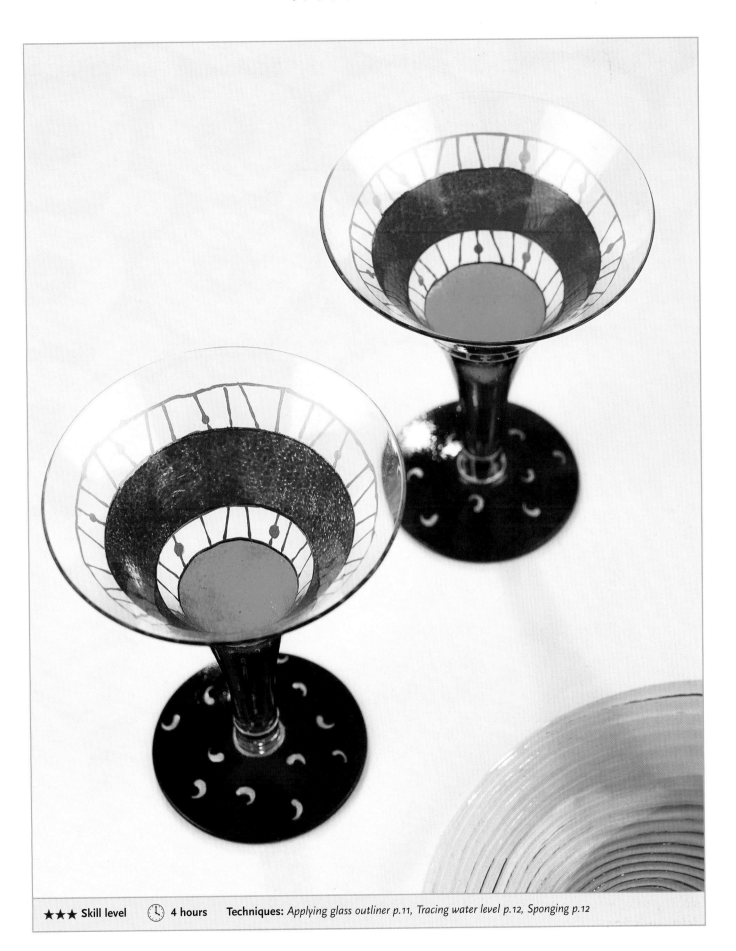

★★★ Skill level   🕐 4 hours   **Techniques:** *Applying glass outliner p.11, Tracing water level p.12, Sponging p.12*

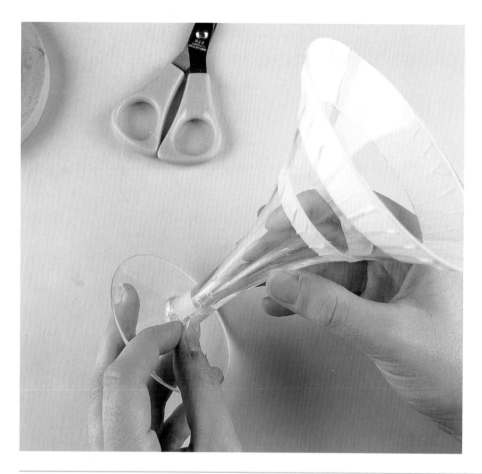

3 Stick a second length of the narrower tape around the stem just above the base. Press all the tapes down well.

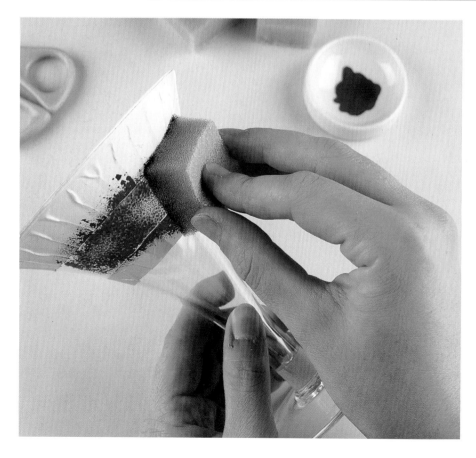

4 With a pair of scissors, cut a piece of synthetic sponge into three chunks about 2.5 cm (1 in) square. Apply pink paint to a piece of sponge with a flat artist's paintbrush. Dab the paint on the masked-off band around the bowl of the glass.

Helpful hint
Cocktail glasses are often made of fine glass so do not bake them to fix the paints unless you are sure they can take the heat of the oven. Handle and hand wash glassware carefully.

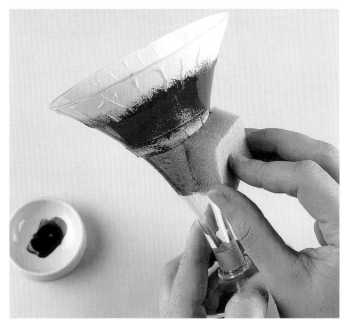

5   Paint another piece of sponge with turquoise paint. Dab the paint onto the stem then sponge the base with purple paint, using a clean piece of sponge. Peel off the masking tape and leave the paints to dry.

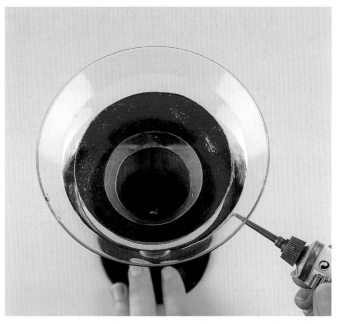

6   Run a line of gold glass outliner along the edges of the masked bands. Pour water into the glass until it is 1 cm (½ in) below the rim. Use the water level as a guide to run a line of outliner around the glass. Pour away the water.

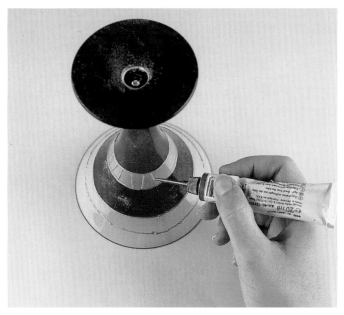

7   Draw random lines across the unpainted bands with the outliner. Apply a dot of outliner on some of the lines.

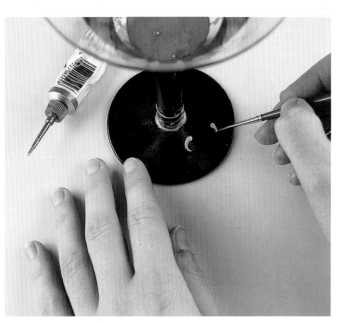

8   Apply a dot of outliner on the base. Use a fine paintbrush to draw out the dot at one edge to make a crescent shape. Continue to decorate the base in this way. Set aside to dry. Bake following the paint manufacturer's instructions to set the paints.

Wave sponged jug

Paint applied with a natural sponge has a random, open holed effect and suits this nautical themed jug with its blue sponged waves and row of pebbles. The waves are worked with frosted glass paint which has a matt finish.

5 cm (2 in) wide masking tape allows you to mask off large areas. Use overlapping lengths of narrower tape if you do not have any wide tape.

You will need

Materials

- 5 cm (2 in) wide masking tape
- Oven-proof clear straight-sided jug, 18 cm (7 in) high
- Bright blue and deep blue frosted glass paints
- White and black ceramic paints

Tools

- Ruler
- Scissors
- Pen
- Craft knife
- Old plate or ceramic tile
- Flat artist's paintbrush
- Natural sponge
- White spirit (if using oil-based paints)
- Medium artist's paintbrush

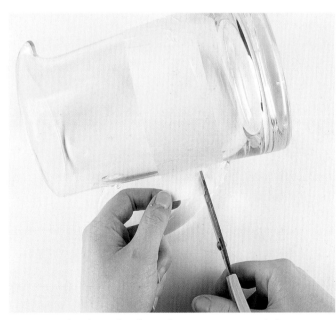

1 Stick a length of masking tape around the jug 5 cm (2 in) above the base. Snip away the excess tape around the handle so the tape fits smoothly. It does not matter if the tape creases as long as it adheres well to the glass.

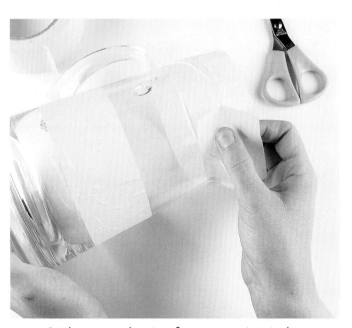

2 Stick a second strip of tape 5 cm (2 in) above the first, pleating it at the spout and trimming it to fit around the handle if necessary. It doesn't have to be absolutely level. Mask off the end of the handle with tape. Tuck excess tape inside the top of the jug.

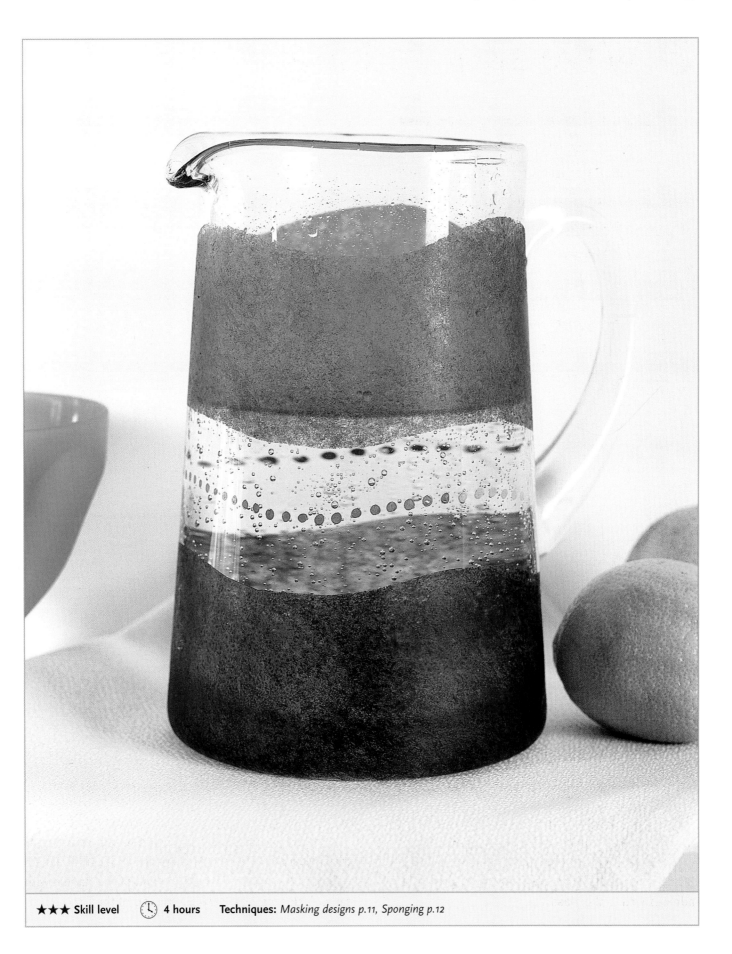

★★★ **Skill level**   🕐 **4 hours**   **Techniques:** *Masking designs p.11, Sponging p.12*

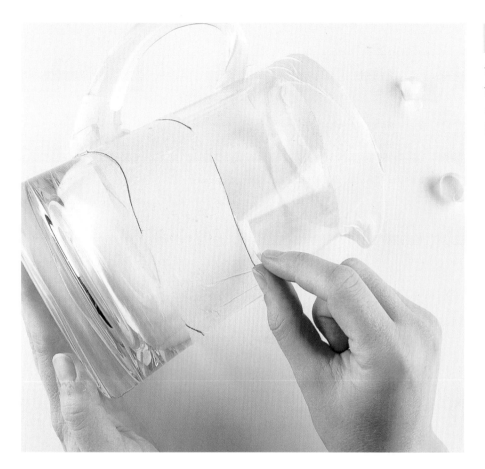

3 With a pen, draw a wavy line along the edges of the tapes except the upper edge of the top piece of tape. Carefully cut along the wavy lines with a craft knife. Peel off the excess tape.

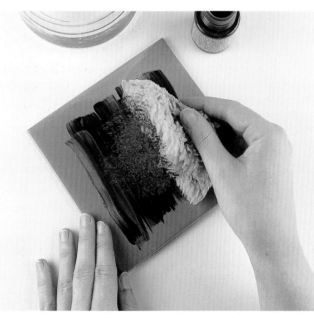

4 Apply bright blue paint to an old plate or ceramic tile (to use as a palette) with a flat artist's paintbrush. Moisten a natural sponge; use white spirit if using oil-based paints or water if using water-based paints. Dab at the paint with the sponge.

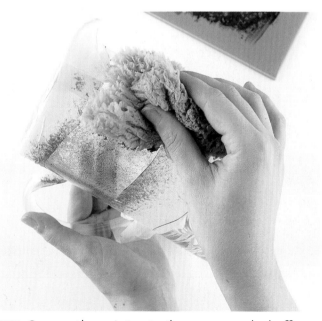

5 Sponge the paint onto the upper masked-off band. Clean the sponge and palette thoroughly.

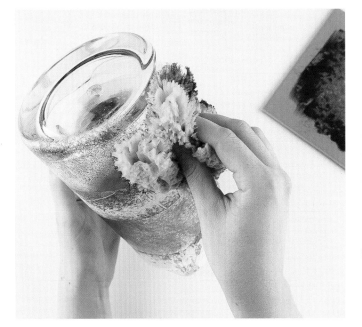

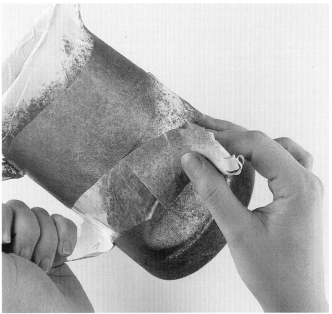

6 Apply deep blue paint to the palette with the paintbrush. Dab at the paint with the sponge. Turn the jug upside down. Holding it by the handle, sponge the paint onto the lower masked-off band.

7 Before the paint dries, peel off the tapes. Make sure you do this carefully as the tapes will have wet paint on them.

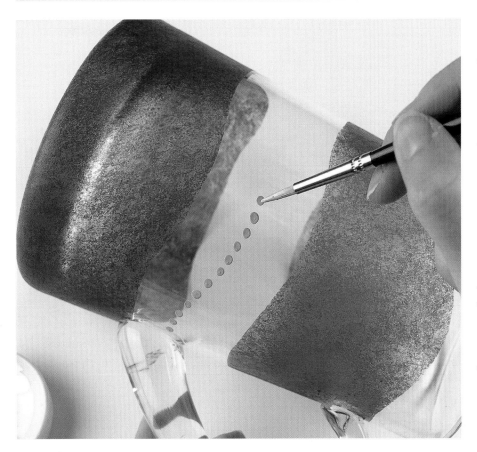

8 Mix white and black ceramic paint together to make grey. With a medium artist's paintbrush, dot the paint in a row between the painted bands. Leave the paint to dry overnight then bake the jug following the paint manufacturer's instructions to set the paints if necessary.

Helpful hint
If you are nervous about dotting the grey paint, draw a line first between the painted bands with a Chinagraph pencil to work along. Wipe away the pencil marks when the paint has dried.

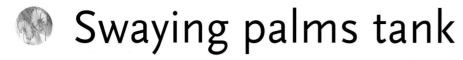

Swaying palms tank

These exotic, stylized palms are outlined with silver outliner and the leaves shaded with white and cool blue glass paints. Concentrating the design at the top of the tank stops it from looking too busy as all the sides can be seen through the clear glass.

For an understated look, work just a single palm on each face of the tank.

You will need

Materials

- Tracing paper
- Clear oven-proof glass tank
- Masking tape
- Silver glass outliner
- Light green, light blue and white frosted glass paints

Tools

- Scissors
- Black pen
- Medium artist's paintbrush
- Fine artist's paintbrush

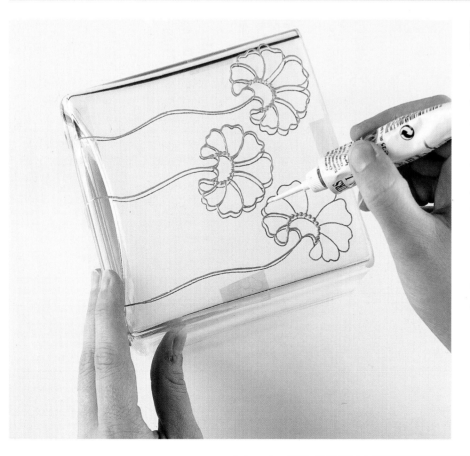

1 Cut a piece of tracing paper to fit behind the front of the tank and another piece to fit behind a side if the tank is rectangular. Trace the palm templates on page 76 onto the tracing paper with a black pen. Stick the tracing behind the front of the tank. Use silver glass outliner to apply a row of dots along the base of the palm leaves, make sure there are no gaps between the dots as paint could seep between them. Trace along all of the outlines with the silver outliner.

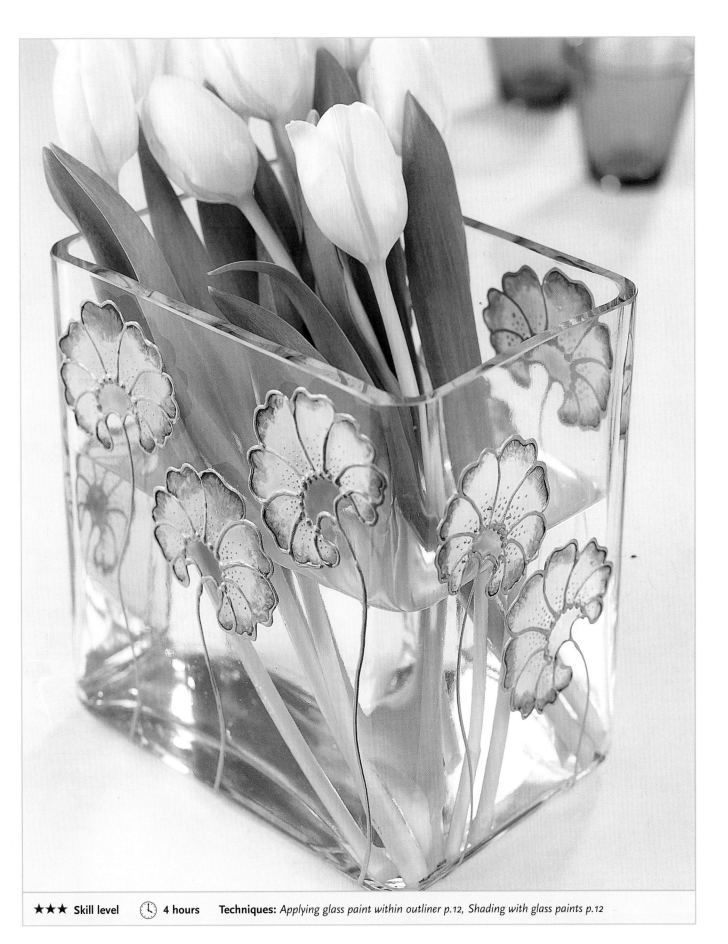

★★★ **Skill level**   🕐 **4 hours**   **Techniques:** *Applying glass paint within outliner p.12, Shading with glass paints p.12*

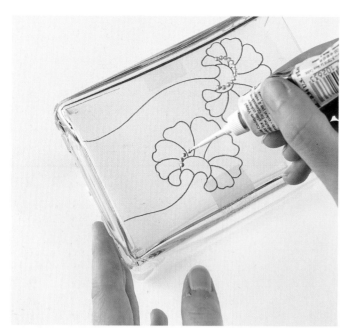

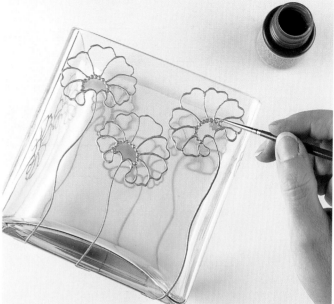

2 Peel the tracing off the front. Stick the tracing for the side of the tank behind one side with masking tape. Dot and trace along the outlines with silver outliner as before. Leave the front and side to dry then repeat on the other faces of the tank.

3 When completely dry, place the front of the tank face up. Using a medium paintbrush, paint the top of the stems light green, pushing the paint into the corners with a fine paintbrush.

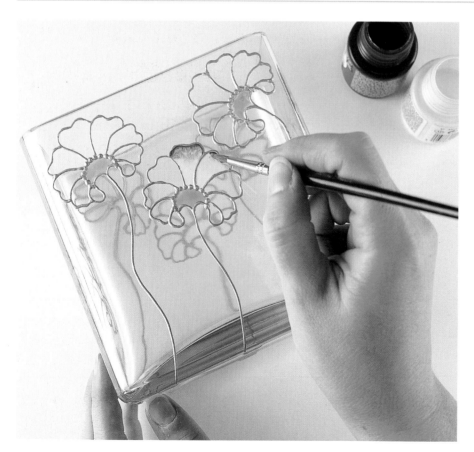

4 Apply light blue paint to the tip of one palm leaf then apply white paint to the rest of the leaf. Blend the colours together to shade the area. Paint all the palms on the front in this way. Leave to dry completely.

Helpful hint
If you are nervous about shading with glass paints, paint the leaves a single colour instead.

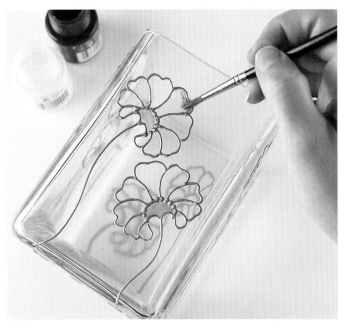

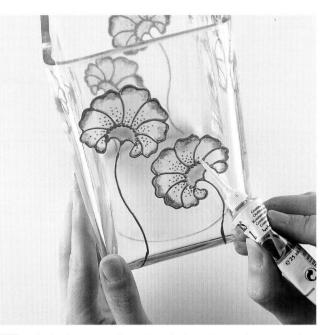

5 Turn the tank to paint a side to match the front. Leave to dry completely then turn the tank to paint the other faces.

6 When the paint has dried, dot the outliner on the lower half of the leaves. Set aside to dry then bake the tank according to the paint manufacturer's instructions to fix the paints if necessary.

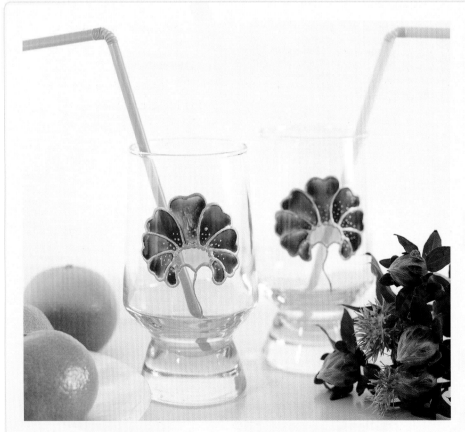

Variation

Palm tumblers

Draw single palms on a pair of drinking glasses. Outline them in gold and colour in a warm yellow and orange colour scheme.

Embellished photo border

Clip frames are plain, inexpensive photo frames but their basic design is ideal for decorating with glass paints. Here, a deep border has been created and brightly coloured. Shiny glass cabochon jewellery stones are applied as a flamboyant finishing touch.

This clip frame is a versatile size. A standard 15 x 10 cm (6 x 4 in) photograph fits the aperture of the colourful border.

You will need

Materials

- Tracing paper
- 25 x 20 cm (10 x 8 in) clip photo frame
- Silver glass outliner
- Colourless, jade green, pink, purple and bright green transparent glass paints
- Selection of cabochon jewellery stones
- White paper

Tools

- Black felt-tip pen
- Medium artist's paintbrush
- Fine artist's paintbrush
- Super glue

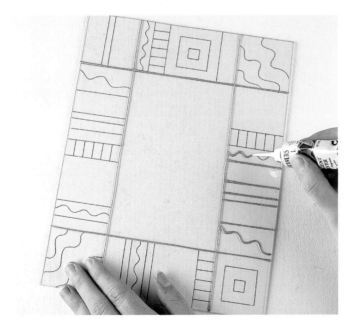

1 Trace the template on page 77 onto tracing paper with a black pen. Remove the backing board from the photo frame and place the glass on the template. Run a line of silver outliner along the inner lines and divisions of the border.

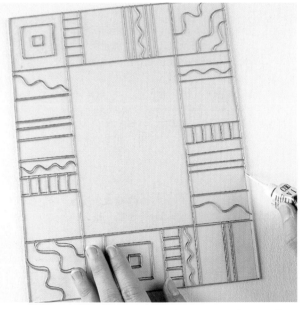

2 Run a line of outliner along the outer edges of the glass. Leave the outliner to dry and remove the tracing.

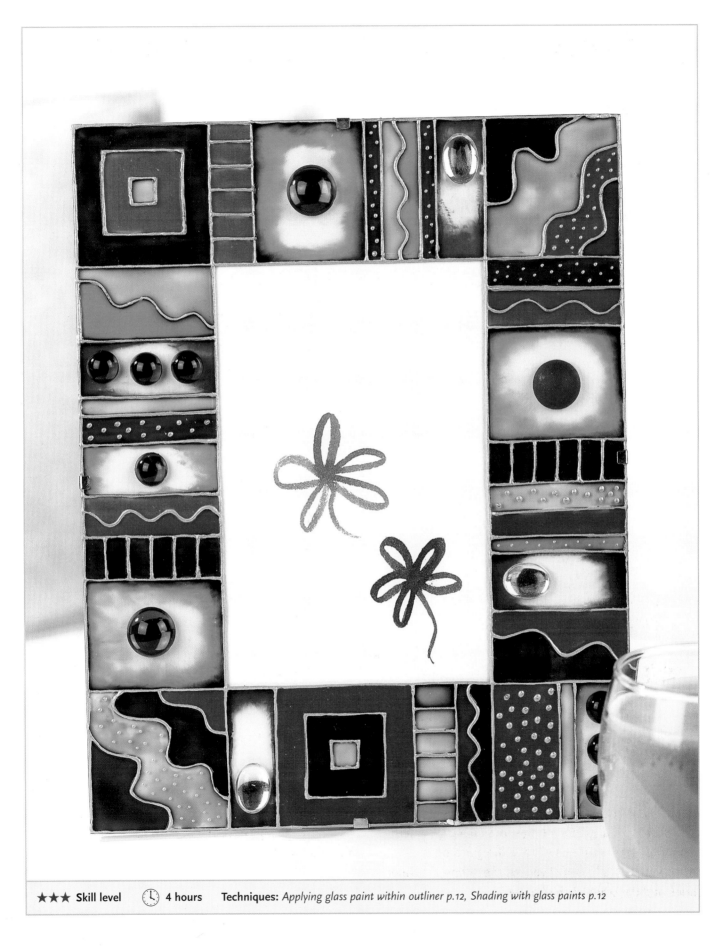

★★★ **Skill level**   🕐 **4 hours**   **Techniques:** *Applying glass paint within outliner p.12, Shading with glass paints p.12*

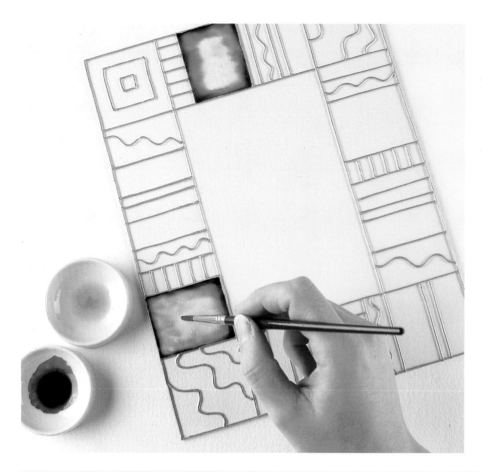

3 Decide which rectangles you would like to place the jewellery stones in. Apply colourless paint to the centre of one of these rectangles with a medium artist's paintbrush. Apply coloured paint to the outer edges and blend the paints together. Paint the other rectangles that will have stones in in the same way.

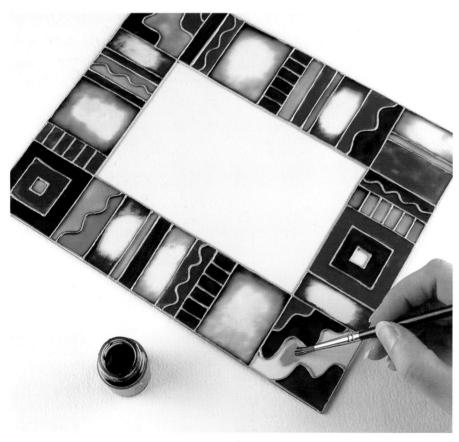

4 Paint the remaining sections in a variety of colours, using a fine artist's paintbrush to brush the paint into tight corners. Leave the photo border to dry.

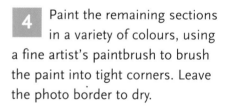

Helpful hint
Consider where you are placing the different colours so there is a good balance over the whole border.

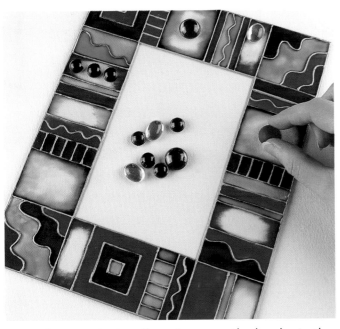

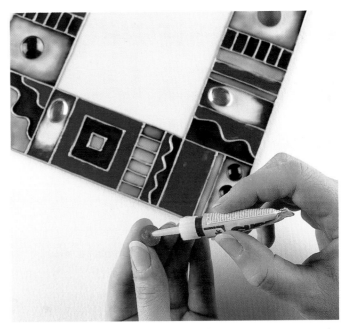

5 Arrange the jewellery stones on the border in the rectangles with colourless centres.

6 When you are happy with the arrangement, stick the stones in place with super glue.

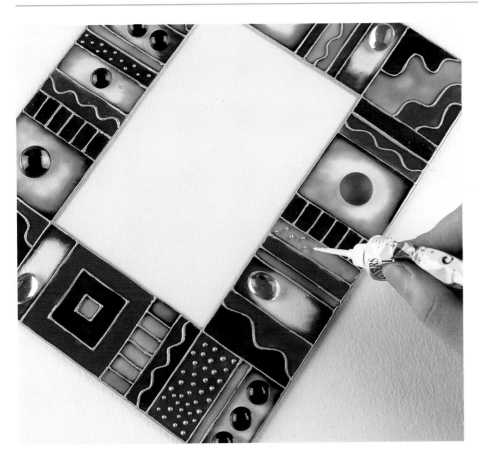

7 As a finishing touch, dot outliner on a few sections of the border. Leave the frame to dry then reassemble it with your choice of display material.

Helpful hint
Stick the photograph or picture in the centre of a piece of white paper cut to the size of the glass with spray glue.

Pin-striped oil bottle

The smart pin-stripes on this oil bottle are easy to draw with a glass painting pen. A simple motif of a sprig of olives painted with frosted paints declare the bottle's contents.

A matching set of kitchen storage bottles would look great decorated with suitable motifs, herbs and chilli peppers for example.

You will need

Materials

- 5 cm (2 in) wide masking tape
- Oven-proof clear glass oil bottle with flat sides
- Sheet of lined paper
- Blue frosted glass painting pen
- Blue, purple and green frosted glass paints
- Kitchen towel

Tools

- Scissors
- Cutting mat
- Black pen
- Metal ruler
- Craft knife
- Chinagraph pencil
- Palette
- Medium artist's paintbrush

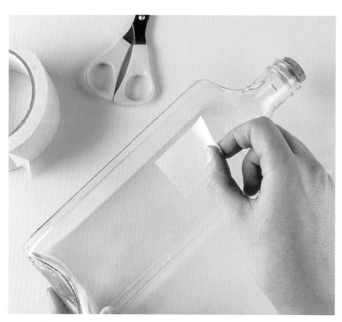

1 Cut a 3.5 cm (1³⁄₈ in) length of masking tape. Stick the tape to the front of the bottle in a central position near the top with the long edges vertical.

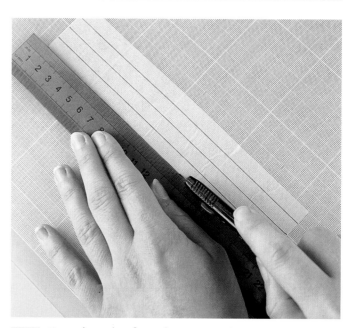

2 Cut a length of masking tape about 2.5 cm (1 in) longer than the flat sides of the bottle. Stick the tape to a cutting mat. Divide into 1 cm (³⁄₈ in) wide strips using a black pen and metal ruler. Cut along the divisions with a craft knife against a metal ruler. Peel off and discard one strip.

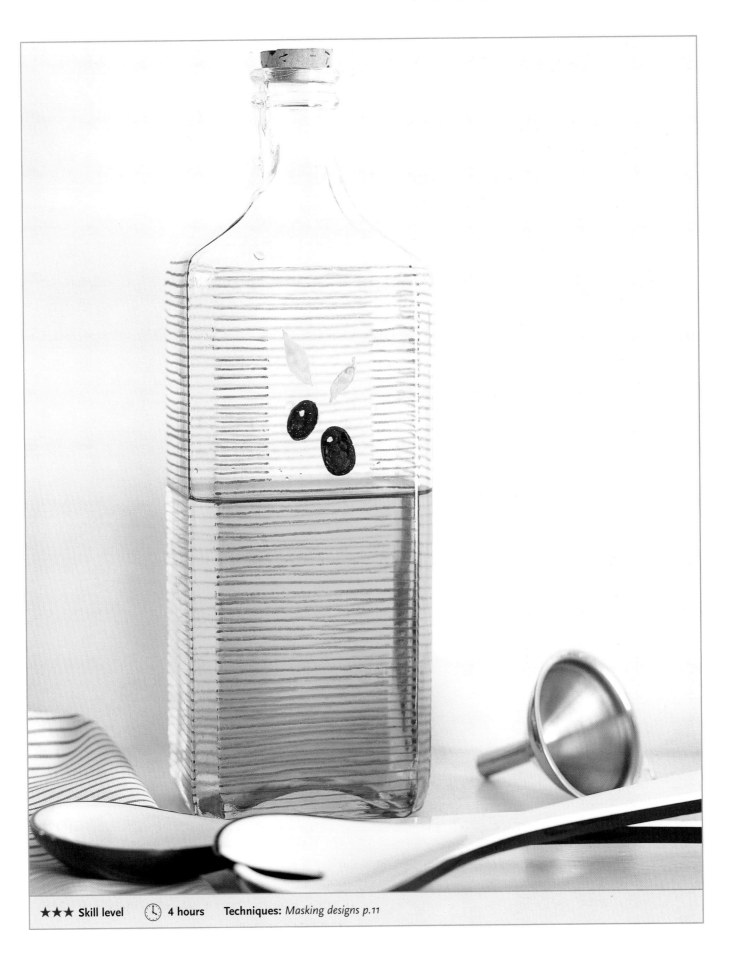

★★★ **Skill level** 🕐 **4 hours** **Techniques:** *Masking designs p.11*

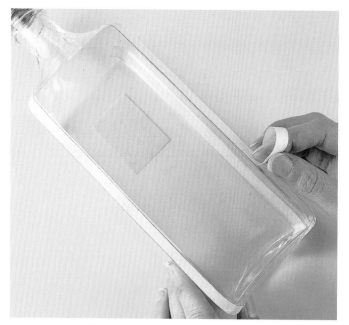

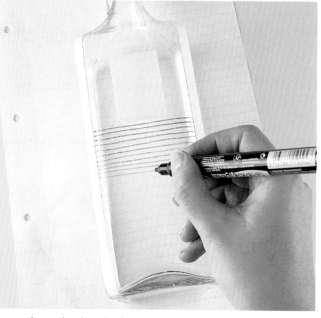

3 Peel off one strip and stick it along one edge of the front. Repeat on the other edges of the bottle. This bottle has slanted corners, so on a bottle with right angled corners have the long edges extending equally on each side of the corner.

4 Place the bottle face up on a sheet of lined paper to use as a guide to keep the drawn lines level. Draw lines about 3 mm (⅛ in) apart across the front with a blue frosted glass painting pen.

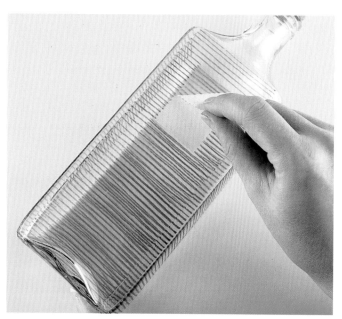

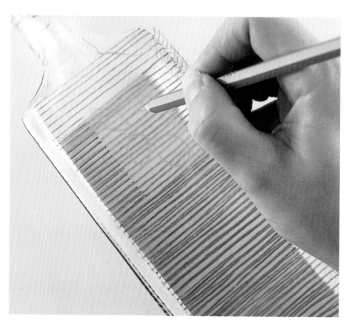

5 Turn the bottle on one side and draw lines across the side that is face up. Leave to dry, then turn the bottle to continue applying the lines. Set the bottle aside whilst the lines dry. Peel off the tapes.

6 With a Chinagraph pencil, draw the olives and leaves freehand in the gap on the front of the bottle or copy the template on page 76.

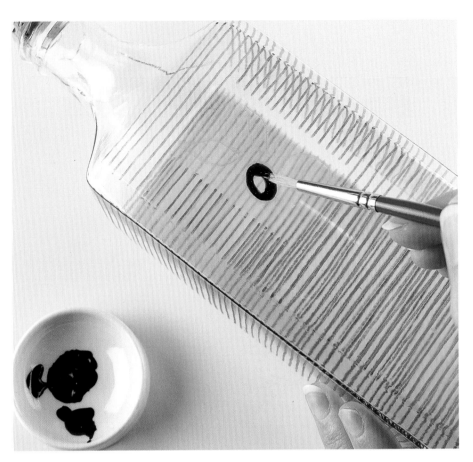

7 Mix blue and purple frosted glass paints together on a palette. Paint the olives, leaving an unpainted area on each as a highlight.

Helpful hint
Don't worry if you forget to leave an unpainted highlight on the olives. Before the paint dries, lift off an area of paint with a clean paintbrush.

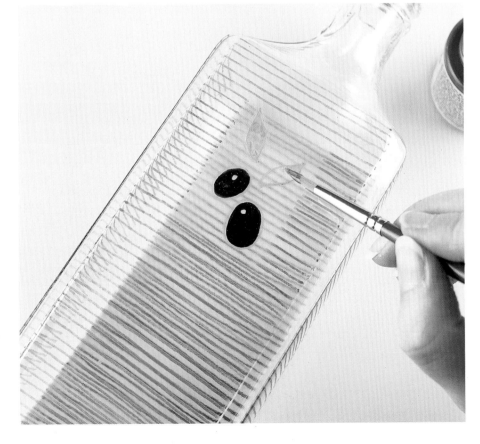

8 Paint the leaves with green frosted glass paint. Leave to dry. Wipe away any visible pencil lines with a kitchen towel. If necessary bake the bottle following the paint manufacturer's instructions to fix the paint.

Templates

*Templates shown are all full size
unless otherwise stated.*

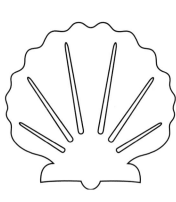

↑ **Frosted shell jar**
(pages 22-25)

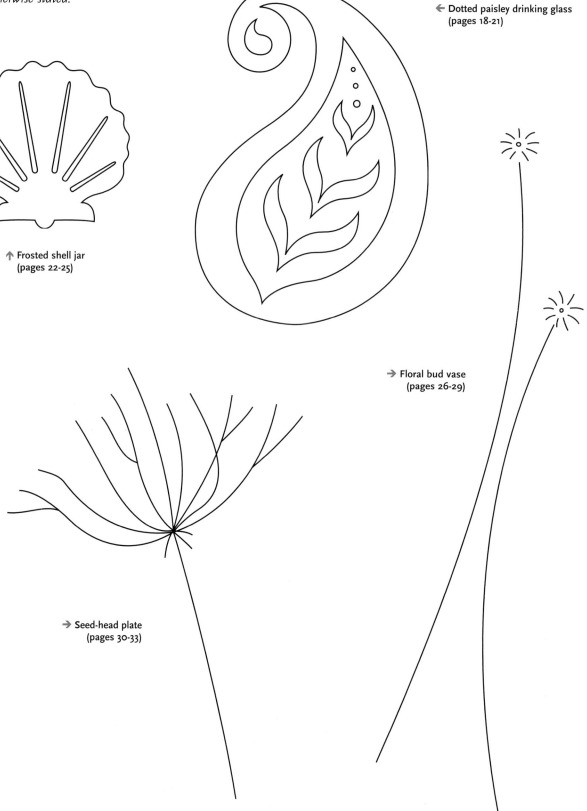

← **Dotted paisley drinking glass**
(pages 18-21)

→ **Floral bud vase**
(pages 26-29)

→ **Seed-head plate**
(pages 30-33)

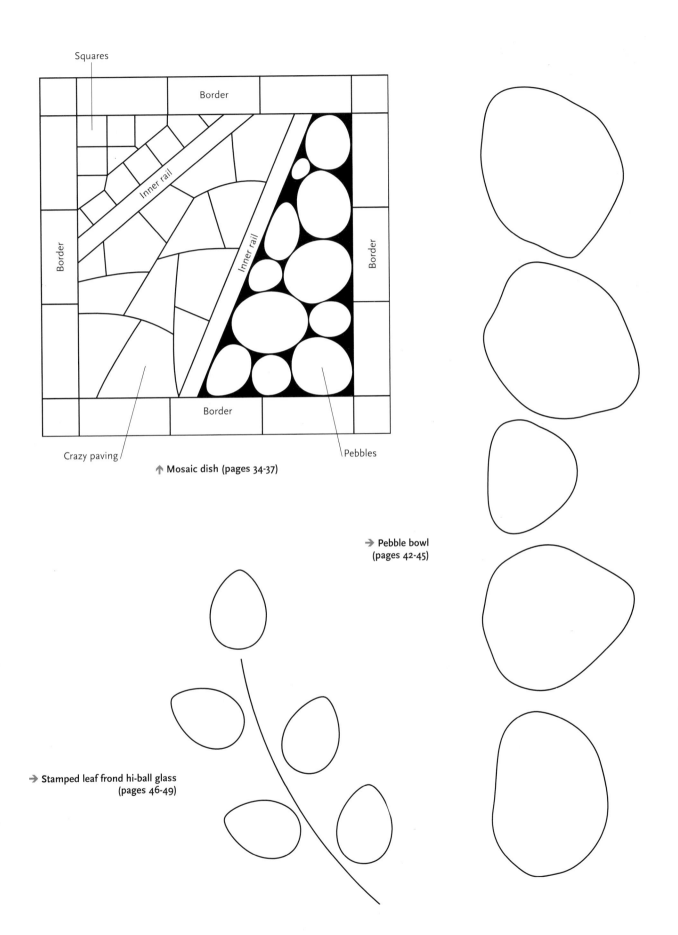

Squares

Border

Inner rail

Inner rail

Border

Border

Border

Crazy paving

Pebbles

↑ Mosaic dish (pages 34-37)

→ Pebble bowl
(pages 42-45)

→ Stamped leaf frond hi-ball glass
(pages 46-49)

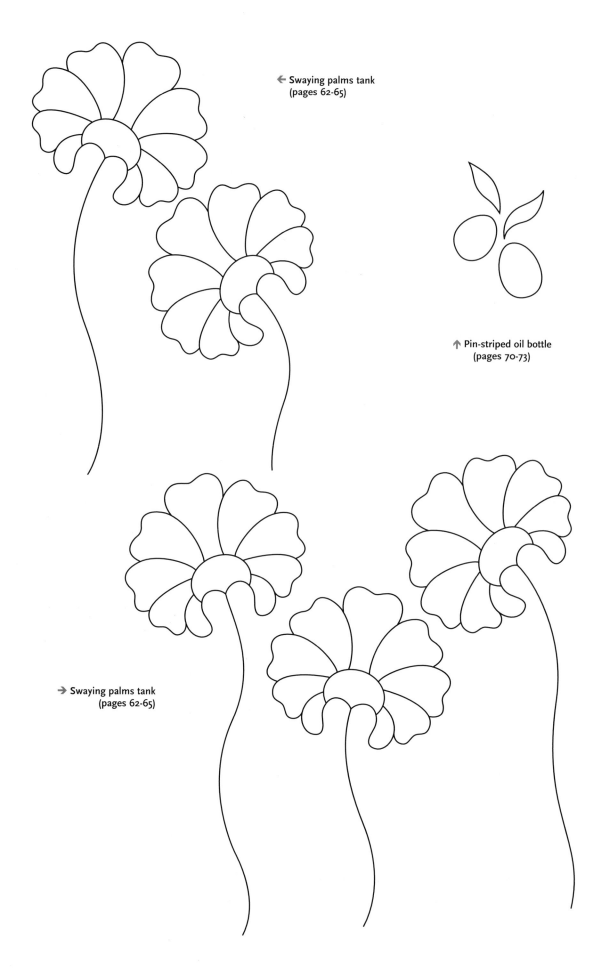

← Swaying palms tank
(pages 62-65)

↑ Pin-striped oil bottle
(pages 70-73)

→ Swaying palms tank
(pages 62-65)

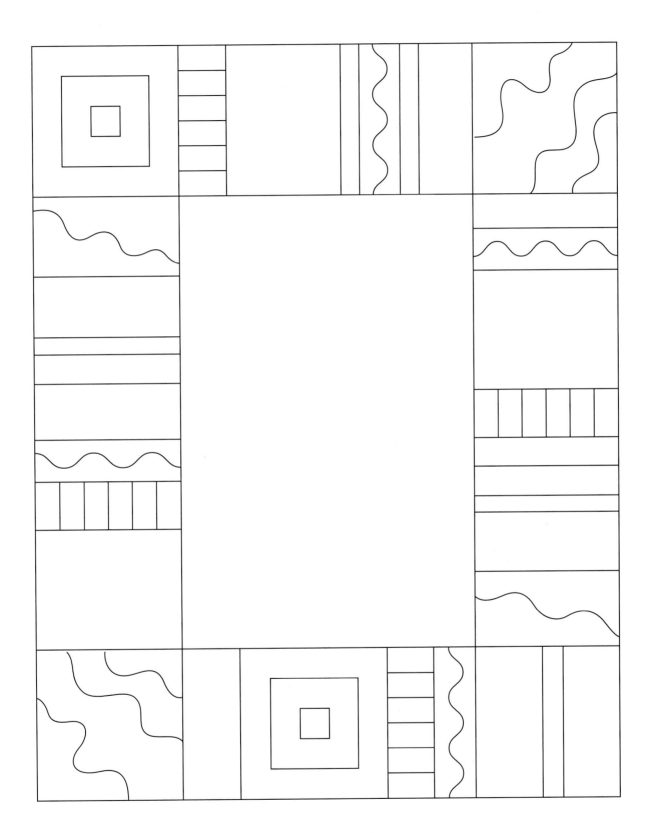

↑ Embellished photo border
(pages 66-69)
Set photocopier to 125% to copy image to correct size for project

Suppliers

UNITED KINGDOM

Craft Depot
Somerton Business Park
Somerton
Somerset TA11 6SB
Tel: 01458 274727
Fax: 01458 272932
Email: craftdepot@aol.com
www.craftdepot.co.uk
Online general craft supplier.

Forbo CP Ltd
Station Rd
Cramlington
Northumberland NE23 8AQ
Tel: 01670 718300
Supplier of sticky-backed plastic, contact for nearest stockist.

Fred Aldous
37 Lever Street
Manchester M1 1LW
Tel: 08707 517 300
www.fredaldous.co.uk
Shop and mail-order for glassware and paints.

The Glass Painting Specialists
www.glasspainter.demon.co.uk
Mail-order company.

Hobbicraft
40 Woodhouse Lane
Merrion Centre
Leeds LS2 8LX
Tel: 0113 2930636
www.hobbicraft.co.uk
Shop and online general craft supplier.

Hobbycraft
www.hobbycraft.co.uk
Branches throughout the UK, supplier of glass paints and general craft equipment.

Homecrafts Direct
Unit 2, Wanlip Rd, Syston
Leicester
Leicestershire LE7 1PD
Tel: 0116 269 7733
Email: info@homecrafts.co.uk
www.homecrafts.co.uk
Mail-order for glassware and paints.

John Lewis Partnership
Tel: 08456 049049
www.johnlewis.com
Branches throughout the UK, supplier of glassware.

Just Glass Paint
29 Station St
Lewes
East Sussex BN7 2DB
Tel: 01273 487670
www.just-glass-paint.co.uk
Online supplier of glass paints.

Laine's Floral Art and Hobby Crafts
60 Commerce Street
Insch
Aberdeenshire AB52 6JB
Tel: 01464 820335
Fax: 0870 1338209
Email: sales@lainesworld.co.uk
www.lainesworld.com
Specialize in Pebeo range of paints. Retail outlet and online shopping.

London Art Limited
132 Finchley Road
London NW3 5HS
Tel: 08707 606286
Email: info@londonart-shop.co.uk
www.londonart-shop.co.uk
Painting and drawing materials. Retail outlet and online shopping.

Millers Art
28 Stockwell Street
Glasgow G1 4RT
Tel: 0141 5531660
Fax: 0141 5531583
Email: sales@millers-art.co.uk
www.millers-art.co.uk
Sell range of glass paints online.

Panduro Hobby
Westway House
Transport Avenue
Brentford
Middlesex TW8 9HF
Tel: 020 8847 6161
www.panduro.co.uk
Mail-order for glassware and paints.

Pebeo
www.pebeo.com
Paint brand sold in outlets throughout the UK.

Rainbow Glass
85 Walkden Road
Worsley
Manchester M28 7BQ
Tel: 0161 7903025
Fax: 0161 6615787
Email: admin@rainbowglass.co.uk
www.glasspaintingmaterials.co.uk
Sell paints, outliners, painting film etc. and wide variety of items to paint on online.

Yorkshire Art Store
10 Market Place
Pickering
YO18 7AA
Tel: 01751 475660
Email: info@yorkshireartstore.co.uk
www.yorkshireartstore.co.uk
Glass paints, outliners and accessories. Retail outlet and online shopping.

AUSTRALIA

Artery
137–141 Collins Street
Hobart TAS 7000
Tel: 03 6234 3788

A-Way To Craft
27 Colbee Court
Phillip ACT 2606
Tel: 02 6281 0193

Eckersley's Arts, Crafts & Imagination
91–93 Edward Street
Brisbane QLD 4000

Glass Craft Australia
54–56 Lexton Road
Box Hill North VIC 3129
Tel: 03 9897 4188

Oxford Art Supplies
145 Victoria Avenue
Chatswood NSW 2067
Tel: 02 9417 8572

Premier Art Supplies Pty Ltd
43 Gilles Street
Adelaide S.A. 5000
Tel: 08 8212 5922
Fax: 08 8231 0441

Yee's Hobbies & Crafts Pty Ltd
19 Bishop Street
Stuart Park NT 0820
Tel: 08 8981 3255

NEW ZEALAND

Brush-N-Palette Artists Supplies Ltd
50 Lichfield Street
Christchurch
Tel/Fax: (03) 366 3088

Gordon Harris Art Supplies
4 Gillies Ave
Newmarket

Auckland
Tel: 09 520 4466
Fax: 09 520 0880
and
31 Symonds St
Auckland Central
Tel: 09 377 9992

Littlejohns Art & Graphic Supplies
170 Victoria Street
Wellington
Tel: 04 385 2099
Fax: 04 385 2090

Spotlight Stores
locations throughout New Zealand
Whangarei 09 430 7220
Wairau Park 09 444 0220
Henderson 09 836 0888
Panmure 09 527 0915
Manukau 09 263 6760
Hamilton 07 839 1793
Rotorua 07 343 6901
New Plymouth 06 757 3575
Hastings 06 878 5223
Palmerston North 06 357 6833
Porirua 04 237 0650
Wellington 04 472 5600
Christchurch 03 377 6121
Dunedin 03 477 1478
www.spotlight.net.nz
*Wide range of craft and decorative
painting supplies.*

SOUTH AFRICA

Art, Stock & Barrel
Shop 44, Parklane Centre
12 Commercial Road
Pietermaritzburg 3201
Tel: 033 342-1026

Centurion Kuns
Shop 45, Eldoraigne Shopping Mall
Saxby Road
Eldoraigne
0157

Pretoria
Tel: 012 654 0449

Crafty Arts
Walmer Park Shopping Centre
Port Elizabeth 6001
Tel: 041 368-2528

Crafty Supplies
Shop UG 2, Stadium on Main
Claremont 7700
Cape Town
Tel: 021 671-0286

East Rand Mall Stationery and Art
Shop 140, East Rand Mall
1459
Johannesburg
Tel: 011 823 1688

L & P Stationery and Art
141 Zastron Street
Westdene
Bloemfontein 9301
Tel: 051 430 1085

Index